SIOUX • Harrison

DAWES • Chadron

SHERIDAN • Rushville

CHERRY • Valentine

KEYA PAHA • Springview

BOYD • Butte

KNOX • Center

CEDAR • Hartington

DIXON • Ponca

DAKOTA • Dakota City

BOX BUTTE • Alliance

BROWN • Ainsworth

ROCK

HOLT • O'Neill

ANTELOPE • Neligh

PIERCE • Pierce

WAYNE • Wayne

THURSTON • Pender

SCOTTS BLUFF • Gering

MORRILL • Bridgeport

GARDEN • Oshkosh

GRANT • Hyannis

HOOKER • Mullen

THOMAS • Thedford

BLAINE • Brewster

LOUP • Taylor

GARFIELD • Burwell

WHEELER • Bartlett

BOONE • Albion

MADISON • Madison

STANTON • Stanton

CUMING • West Point

BURT • Tekamah

BANNER • Harrisburg

ARTHUR • Arthur

MCPHERSON • Tryon

LOGAN • Stapleton

CUSTER • Broken Bow

VALLEY • Ord

GREELEY • Greeley

NANCE • Fullerton

PLATTE • Columbus

COLFAX • Schuyler

DODGE • Fremont

WASHINGTON • Blair

KIMBALL • Kimball

CHEYENNE • Sidney

DEUEL • Chappell

KEITH • Ogallala

LINCOLN • North Platte

SHERMAN • Loup City

HOWARD • St Paul

MERRICK • Central City

POLK • Osceola

BUTLER • David City

SAUNDERS • Wahoo

DOUGLAS • Omaha

SARPY • Papillion

PERKINS • Grant

DAWSON • Lexington

BUFFALO • Kearney

HALL • Grand Island

HAMILTON • Aurora

YORK • York

SEWARD • Seward

LANCASTER • LINCOLN

CASS • Plattsmouth

OTOE • Nebraska City

CHASE • Imperial

HAYES • Hayes Center

FRONTIER • Stockville

GOSPER • Elwood

PHELPS • Holdrege

KEARNEY • Minden

ADAMS • Hastings

CLAY • Clay Center

FILLMORE • Geneva

SALINE • Wilber

GAGE • Beatrice

JOHNSON • Tecumseh

NEMAHA • Auburn

DUNDY • Benkelman

HITCHCOCK • Trenton

RED WILLOW • McCook

FURNAS • Beaver City

HARLAN • Alma

FRANKLIN • Franklin

WEBSTER • Red Cloud

NUCKOLLS • Nelson

THAYER • Hebron

JEFFERSON • Fairbury

PAWNEE • Pawnee City

RICHARDSON • Falls City

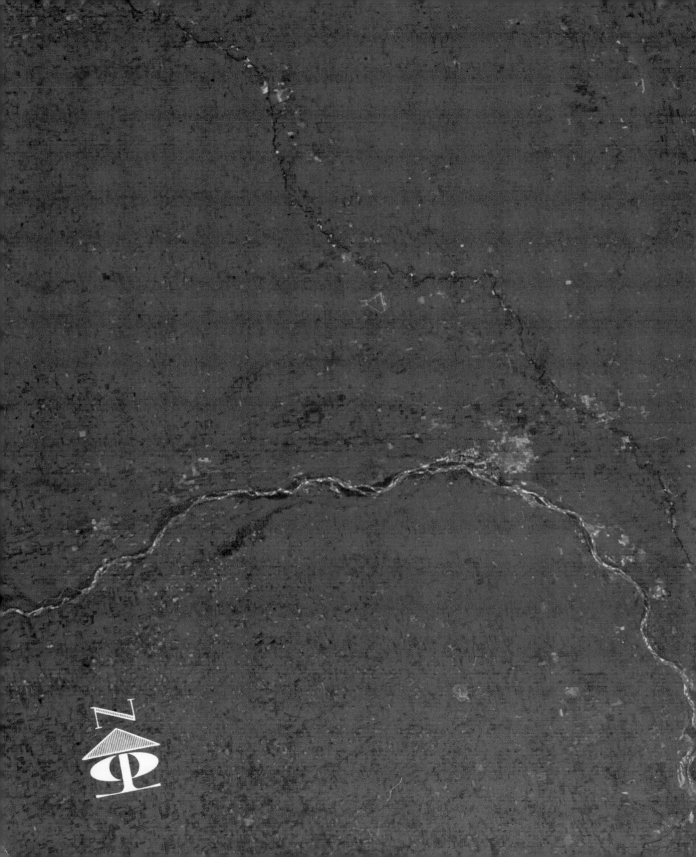

The New

Enchantment of America

NEBRASKA

By Allan Carpenter

 CHILDRENS PRESS, CHICAGO

ACKNOWLEDGMENTS

For assistance in the preparation of the revised edition, the author thanks:
DON A. ATWATER, Public Information Director, Nebraska Department of Economic Development.

American Airlines—Anne Vitaliano, Director of Public Relations; *Capitol Historical Society*, Washington, D.C.; *Newberry Library,* Chicago, Dr. Lawrence Towner, Director; *Northwestern University Library*, Evanston, Illinois; *United Airlines*—John P. Grember, Manager of Special Promotions; Joseph P. Hopkins, Manager, News Bureau.

UNITED STATES GOVERNMENT AGENCIES: *Department of Agriculture*—Robert Hailstock, Jr., Photography Division, Office of Communication; Donald C. Schuhart, Information Division, Soil Conservation Service. *Army*—Doran Topolosky, Public Affairs Office, Chief of Engineers, Corps of Engineers. *Department of Interior*—Louis Churchville, Director of Communications; EROS Space Program—Phillis Wiepking, Community Affairs; Charles Withington, Geologist; Mrs. Ruth Herbert, Information Specialist; Bureau of Reclamation; National Park Service—Fred Bell and the individual sites; Fish and Wildlife Service—Bob Hines, Public Affairs Office. *Library of Congress*—Dr. Alan Fern, Director of the Department of Research; Sara Wallace, Director of Publications; Dr. Walter W. Ristow, Chief, Geography and Map Division; Herbert Sandborn, Exhibits Officer. *National Archives*—Dr. James B. Rhoads, Archivist of the United States; Albert Meisel, Assistant Archivist for Educational Programs; David Eggenberger, Publications Director; Bill Leary, Still Picture Reference; James Moore, Audio-Visual Archives. *United States Postal Service*—Herb Harris, Stamps Division.

For assistance in the preparation of the first edition, the author thanks:
Robert N. Manley, Professor of History, The Hiram Scott College, Scottsbluff, Nebraska; Frank B. Morrison, Governor; John E. Lynch, Executive Secretary, Nebraska State Education Association; Nebraskaland, Game, Forestation and Parks Commission, Lincoln; Dick Schaffer, Editor, *Nebraskaland* Magazine; Committee for National Arbor Day, West Orange, New Jersey.

Illustrations on the preceding pages:
Cover photograph: Windmill at Sunset, Jim Rowan
Page 1: Commemorative stamps of historic interest
Pages 2-3: Chimney Rock National Historic Site, Oregon Trail landmarks, USDI, NPS, from Oregon Trail Museum Association
Page 3 (Map): USDI Geological Survey
Pages 4-5: Omaha area, EROS Space Photo, USDI Geological Survey, EROS Data Center

Project Editor, Revised Edition:
 Joan Downing
Assistant Editor, Revised Edition:
 Mary Reidy

Library of Congress Cataloging in Publication Data

Carpenter, John Allan, 1917-
 Nebraska.

 (His The new enchantment of America)
 SUMMARY: Presents the history, resources, famous citizens, and points of interest in the Cornhusker State.
 1. Nebraska—Juvenile literature.
[1. Nebraska] I. Title. II. Series: Carpenter, John Allan, 1917- The new enchantment of America.
F666.3.C3 1979   978.2   78-10480
ISBN 0-516-04127-4

Contents

Julius Sterling Morton (right), the founder of Arbor Day, made many other contributions to his nation and his adopted state. He became secretary and then acting governor of the Nebraska Territory, and later secretary of agriculture under President Grover Cleveland. Morton's estate at Nebraska City is now Arbor Lodge State Historical Park (below).

A True Story to Set the Scene

HIS MONUMENTS GROW EVERYWHERE

He had been looking forward to joining the people of Nebraska in the first celebration of its kind ever held; he had, in fact, invented and proposed the celebration and been instrumental in making it official. Yet when the day finally came, its founder was not able to take part in it.

The story of that first celebration, and the extraordinary success it became in later years, is one of the most interesting stories of the enchantment of Nebraska.

Julius Sterling Morton came to Nebraska in 1855 to make his home on a bluff of the Missouri River near Nebraska City, then newly established. The timber along the river did not extend to his acres, so he began at once to plant shade and fruit trees. As his trees grew, Morton also grew in prominence in the Nebraska region. He became convinced that the planting of trees would be one of the greatest blessings for future generations in Nebraska.

In one of his speeches Morton said, "If I had the power, I would compel every man in the state who had a home of his own to plant out and cultivate fruit trees."

In January, 1872, Morton presented the following resolution to the state board of agriculture: "Resolved, That Wednesday, the 10th day of April, 1872, be, and the same is hereby, especially set apart and consecrated for tree planting in the state of Nebraska, and the State Board of Agriculture hereby name it Arbor Day; and to urge upon the people of the State the vital importance of tree planting, hereby offer a special premium of one hundred dollars to the agricultural society of the county in Nebraska which shall, upon that day, plant properly the largest number of trees; and a farm library of twenty-five dollars' worth of books to that person who, on that day, shall plant properly, in Nebraska, the greatest number of trees."

Although some of the board members thought the celebration's name should be "Sylvan Day," they passed the resolution just as it was written.

The first Arbor Day ever celebrated was indeed a fantastic success. About a million trees were planted in the state that day. Ironically, the founder of Arbor Day, J. Sterling Morton, was not able to take part. He had ordered eight hundred trees, but they failed to arrive in time for the celebration. However, he wrote, "They will come soon and then I will put them out." He had put out thousands before and was to plant many more thousands before he died.

On that first Arbor Day, Morton wrote to an Omaha newspaper: "Trees grow in time. The poorest landowner in Nebraska has just as large a fortune of time secured to him as has the richest. And the rain and sunshine and seasons will be his partners, just as genially and gently as they will be those of any millionaire, and will make the trees planted by the poor man grow just as grandly and beautifully as those planted by the opulent. . . .

"The wealthiest and most powerful potentate on earth cannot hire one to speed its growth or bear fruit before its time. . . . There is a true triumph in the unswerving integrity and genuine democracy of trees. . . . Then what infinite beauty and loveliness we can add to the pleasant plains of Nebraska by planting forest and fruit trees upon every swell of their voluptuous undulations, and in another short decade, make her the Orchard of the Union, the Sylvan queen of the Republic."

Morton's interest in trees was a very practical one. They were needed for fuel, lumber, fencing, and many other purposes. Also he felt, as did many others, that forests would hold the rainfall and help make the waste places blossom.

Two years after the first Arbor Day, Morton wrote in his diary: "Arbor Day, an invention of mine, has now become a public holiday, destined to become a blessing to posterity as well as to ourselves. . . . Other holidays repose upon the past; Arbor Day proposes for the future." He could hardly have realized what an extraordinary success his day would become over the years.

Arbor Day is still celebrated at Arbor Lodge, as in this 1970s ceremony with Vern Livingston as honoree (opposite).

Lay of the Land

BEELINE FOR THE BORDER

The great Paul Bunyan had failed miserably to make a straight border for southern Nebraska. He tried to plow a straight line with his blue ox, Babe, but the furrow was very crooked and soon filled up to become the Republican River. However, Nebraska's own great folk hero, Febold Feboldson, was equal to the task. For this purpose, it is said, he devoted fifteen years of his life to crossing eagles with bees. At last he produced great, humming insects as large as the noblest eagle. After some difficulty in making harnesses for them, he finally hitched a couple of the strongest "beeagles" to a plow, and they made a perfect beeline across the country. This, according to the colorful legend, is how the southern Nebraska boundary was formed.

Whatever their origin, all of Nebraska's boundaries are perfectly straight artificial borders, except for the Missouri River line on the east and northeast. Nebraska shares the Missouri River with Missouri, Iowa, and South Dakota. Other neighbors are Wyoming, Colorado, and Kansas.

From its highest point—about a mile high (1.6 kilometers) in western Banner County—Nebraska gently tilts to the east and southwest toward its lowest point, 825 feet (251 meters) above sea level in Richardson County.

Dissected Till Plains cover the eastern fifth of the state. The retreat of the last glacier left a rich layer of soil-forming *till* on the land, which is cut up, or *dissected,* by many streams. The till plains are very good for farming.

The Great Plains cover the rest of the state and extend into Colorado and Wyoming.

Twenty counties in north-central Nebraska are included in what is known as the Sandhills area. This once was the bed of a vast, sandy

Opposite: Chimney Rock, a famous landmark of the Oregon Trail.

sea; then it was laid bare to the elements. Over the eons the sand blew into rolling hills and ridges, constantly changing form. In a very recent period—some say within the time of European exploration—lush grasses began to grow over the sand. Today the rolling slopes are covered with grasses, which hold the sand in place. Except in a few bare spots, the sand no longer changes form as the winds blow. Nebraska's grasslands are said to be different from any other region of the world.

In the west, the flowing plains rise abruptly to merge with the Wildcat Hills. Western bluffs and buttes played a part in America's westward expansion as landmarks for travelers.

Another outstanding natural Nebraska feature is the Badlands region, an extension of the Badlands of South Dakota.

WATERS: FLOWING AND LANDLOCKED

Nebraska takes its name from its outstanding natural feature—the fantastic Platte River. The Omaha Indians called the Platte *Nibathaska;* the Oto Indians named it *Nibrathka.* Both of these words mean "flat, or shallow, water." So Nebraska is literally the land of the flat water. Explorer John C. Frémont said, "The names given by the Indians are always remarkably appropriate; and certainly none was ever more so than that which they have given to this stream—the Nebraska, or Shallow River!"

Near the city of North Platte, the Platte River is formed by the junction of the North Branch, flowing from Wyoming, and the South Branch, flowing from Colorado. The Platte is so broad and so shallow in most places that it has been the subject of many jokes. Humorist Artemus Ward visited the region and said that the Platte would be a good river if set on edge.

About three-fourths of Nebraska is drained by the Platte and its tributaries. Sometimes the waters swell and rage due to spring thaws or rains; other times the river channels are almost dry. The Loup River is the largest tributary of the Platte. Others include the Elkhorn, Cedar, Dismal, and Calamus.

Above: The Platte River at Scotts Bluff, on the Oregon Trail.
Below: A section of the Nebraska Badlands, near Toadstool Park.

No major tributaries flow into the Platte from the south. This was one reason that the Oregon Trail was so easy to follow in Nebraska. There was a minimum of water to cross. The trail followed a north-westerly route along the Little Blue River to its beginning, then continued on to Fort Kearney, on the Platte, where it turned west and followed the south bank of the Platte. The Big Blue River begins not far from the Platte, but instead of flowing into it, flows north, east, and then south into Kansas. The Little Blue flows southeast until it joins the Big Blue in Kansas.

The Republican River flows along much of the southern boundary of Nebraska before leaving the state near Superior. In the north, the Niobrara River runs almost the entire width of the state until it joins the Missouri, the most famous river touching Nebraska.

Altogether, there are about 5,765 miles (9,278 kilometers) of flowing water in the state.

There are about 3,350 major lakes in Nebraska, and innumerable ponds dot the landscape. In the Sandhills area alone, there are about 2,000 shallow lakes. Largest of the state's lakes is McConaughy, formed by Kingsley Dam. There are 17 other major man-made lakes in Nebraska. On the Missouri River, Lewis and Clark Lake is formed by Gavins Point Dam. It is the only one of the man-made Missouri River lakes that touches Nebraska. Other lakes and reservoirs of the state include Hugh Butler (Red Willow), Box Butte, Willow, Sherman, Sutherland, Jeffrey, Enders, Swanson, Harlan County, Medicine Creek, Jefferson, Johnson, and Maloney.

IN ANCIENT AGES

Several times in past ages Nebraska lay at the murky bottom of inland seas. Each time, forces deep inside the earth raised the surface upward, and the sea waters drained off. Sometimes in these "dry" periods, the climate was almost tropical, and tropical plants and animals lived on the land. The most recent upheaval (about sixty million years ago) was the Rocky Mountain uplift, which formed our greatest western range. Nebraska was on the eastern

16

*Morril Hall Museum at the University of Nebraska
is home of the world's largest mammoth skeleton.*

edge of this mighty lifting, and the state was tilted downward to the east as the land to the west rose even higher. None of the great mountains thrust through the surface of Nebraska, as they did in neighboring Colorado, Wyoming, and South Dakota. The new slope of the land made the waters run faster, forming many new streams.

During the ice ages, only two of the great continental glaciers reached what is now Nebraska, and these covered only portions of eastern Nebraska.

STONE BONES

As the seas came and went, the plants, animals, and fish that lived there died. Some of their skeletons turned to stone over the years, becoming what Chief Red Cloud called "stone bones." Nebraska is one of the greatest hunting grounds for these stone bones, or fossils.

An expert named Leidy heard Red Cloud talking about stone bones and began to study them. As early as 1850 he wrote a book about the region's fossils, *Ancient Fauna of Nebraska*. Captain James H. Cook made fossil discoveries at a later date. He established his ranch near the site of his discoveries, now famous as the Agate

Springs Fossil Quarries. Many of the discoveries were housed nearby in the Cook Museum of Natural History. Other famous Nebraska fossil quarries are Devil's Gulch and Hay Springs.

Probably nowhere has a wider variety of fossils been found than in Nebraska. Many fossil creatures had been lost to human memory and could not be identified with any living things. One of these was a huge, shovel-tusked mastodon. Other fossils found in Nebraska include the rhinoceroslike great titanotheres, piglike animals known as oreodonts, and a primitive tusked pig known as donohyus, 6 feet high (1.8 meters). The clumsy relative of the horse called moropus has been found in Nebraska quarries, as well as giant beavers, large turtles, camels, and crocodiles. Paleontologists are positive that more fossils will be found as exploration continues.

CLIMATE

Due to their height, the western tablelands of Nebraska are generally cooler than the eastern plains. However, throughout the state, temperatures vary quickly in a manner common to most far-inland regions. The warm winds known as chinooks, which often blow across northwest Nebraska, make this area somewhat more moderate than the rest of the state during the winter. The number of sunny days is high, and humidity is generally low.

Rainfall varies from about thirty inches (seventy-six centimeters) per year in the southeast to about sixteen inches (forty-one centimeters) in the west. The average rainfall for the state as a whole is about twenty-two inches (fifty-six centimeters). The rains come mostly in May, June, and July, during the best period for crops.

Footsteps on the Land

PREHISTORIC AND PROTOHISTORIC PEOPLES

No spectacular ruins or other such remains of ancient civilizations have been discovered in Nebraska. However, over the years many items have been found that tell about some of the peoples who made the area their home long ago.

The oldest group known to have lived in the Nebraska region was called Folsom people. Their carved arrowheads and spearheads, known as Folsom points, have been unearthed. Because Folsom relics have been found in connection with such fossils as an ancient bison skeleton, it is assumed that these people hunted now-extinct plains animals, such as the mammoth, musk ox, and ancient bison.

Probably there were people in Nebraska before the Folsom culture; there have been many groups since. These include the Sterns Creek, Upper Republican, and Nebraska cultures. Near Plattsmouth have been found relics of the Sterns Creek people. Their carved antelope horns show that they knew how to work in bone; they also made pottery. They apparently grew some crops and made their houses of poles, bark, and reeds. Nebraska culture people left enough bone hoes and other agricultural instruments to show that they were probably good farmers. They also made pottery.

Among the especially interesting prehistoric remains in Nebraska are the ancient flint quarries found near Nehawka. Prehistoric mounds called stone cists are found near O'Neill. These were burial boxes formed from limestone slabs, which were set in shallow dugouts and covered with dirt. Inside the mounds have been found implements, jewelry of bones and shells, stone hatchets, and spearheads.

Ionia "Volcano," near Ponca, is not really a volcano. It is a high bluff on the Missouri River; chemicals in the clay of the bluff react with water and form a smoke or steam. The prehistoric people who lived in the region considered the volcano sacred. Some accounts say that the old, the sick, prisoners of war, or others were tortured and then sacrificed to the gods who controlled the volcano.

After the Indians planted their crops in the spring, they would go off on a major buffalo hunt, as shown in this Currier and Ives picture.

EIGHT TRIBES

Eight major tribes of Indians were found by the first European explorers in Nebraska. They were the Pawnee, Omaha, Oto, Ponca, Sioux, Cheyenne, Arapahoe, and Missouri.

The Pawnee were present in the largest numbers. As late as 1800 there were estimated to be more than ten thousand living in what is now Nebraska. They were primarily farmers, raising beans, corn, and melons as well as tobacco. After the women planted the crops in the spring, the whole group would go off on a major buffalo hunt, and the crops would have to care for themselves. The Pawnee built circular lodges, sometimes as much as 60 feet (18.3 meters) in diameter. The floor was generally below ground level. In the center was a crude fireplace. The smoke escaped through a hole in the roof. The supports of logs were covered with mud to make firm walls.

The village formed the important unit of tribal organization. The village council was made up of chiefs, who inherited their title, and other leaders of the village. Medicine men were charged with the care of the sacred objects of the village and with the many ceremonials. Tribes were made up of several villages, with a tribal council of representatives from the village councils. The entire Pawnee nation was governed by a grand council made up of the members of the various tribal councils. The great united Pawnee nation included the following principal divisions: Kitkehaki (Republican Pawnee), Chaui (Grand Pawnee), Skidi (Loup or Wolf Pawnee), and Pitahauerat (Noisy Pawnee).

Buffalo hunts were organized by tribes, and there were officials who kept order and took charge of the distribution of the meat so that no family was left out. The meat was cut in narrow strips, dried by a process called *jerking,* and stored in containers called *parfleches.*

The Pawnee were noted for their elaborate ceremonials. Almost every daily activity was observed with some kind of ceremony.

All hair on the braves' heads was shaved off except for a narrow ridge of hair over the top of the head; this scalp lock was known as a *pariki.* Some form of the word *pariki* may have given the Pawnee their name. Hair of the women was tightly woven into two braids worn down the back; they reddened the scalp at the part in their hair as well as their cheeks.

Most of the other Indian tribes found by early explorers in Nebraska were smaller in number and had migrated to the area in comparatively recent times. The Omaha were among the most gentle and friendly. They had no war chiefs and seldom fought. However, one of their chiefs, Blackbird, was known for his cruelty to his own people. According to legend, he poisoned many who opposed him. Blackbird started the pirate custom, later followed by the Sioux, of stopping travelers on the Missouri and trying to collect a fee before letting them proceed. He died during a plague of smallpox that killed many of the Indians of the region.

Working closely with the Europeans, the Omaha nation was served by many notable and worthy leaders. Big Elk was one of America's most far-seeing chiefs. He did a great deal to prepare his people for European rule, which he saw could not be avoided. He adopted a son, Iron Eye (Joseph La Flesche), who was part Ponca and part French. Iron Eye succeeded him. Big Elk ruled his tribe with wisdom. When the Winnebago were driven out of their traditional homes in the north and east, the Omaha kindly took in some groups of them and gave them land.

The Ponca were considered among the most successful of all Indian farmers of the region. The Missouri and Oto were related tribes of Sioux background. The principal Oto village, near present Ashland, had about two hundred lodges of earthen construction. Like the Omaha, the Oto were a peaceful people. They were also noted for their burial customs. Old women of the Oto tribe dug graves only large enough to hold the bodies in a sitting position, and the same old women conducted the funeral services. The grave opening was covered with sticks and a buffalo robe, and then dirt was piled on top. Often a pony would be strangled and left on the grave for the coyotes and carrion birds. The bleached pony skull would be placed on the grave as a marker, along with the tail hairs, tied to a stick. When graves could not be dug, the dead were placed in the limbs of trees. Some oak trees near the Oto villages were found to contain many Indian mummies, wrapped in animal skins and tied tightly to tree limbs.

More nomadic and aggressive were the Indians of the western plains of Nebraska—Arapahoe, Cheyenne, and the fierce Sioux. These plains Indians considered most of the state their hunting ground. They terrified not only the European settlers but also the Indians to the east. War between the Pawnee and the Sioux almost never ceased. The Pawnee also kept up running battles with the Crow, Arapahoe, Cheyenne, Osage, Comanche, and Kiowa.

CASUAL VISITS

Tales of a great city, its streets paved with gold, lured Spanish explorer Coronado into the American plains in 1541. He once was thought to be the first European to set foot on what is now Nebraska, though recent research discredits the notion. Spanish explorer-colonizer Don Juan de Oñate may have visited Nebraska in 1598.

22

When the English colonies of Virginia, Connecticut, and Massachusetts were established on the eastern coast of America, they claimed that their territory extended as far west as the western seas. If the claim had been allowed, it would have put the future city of Omaha in Connecticut.

Explorer Robert Cavalier, Sieur de La Salle, claimed vast regions of America, including Nebraska, for France. The Spanish did not recognize these claims, and it appears that groups of both French and Spanish wandered through the region for many generations. The French helped their Pawnee Indian allies in the area, and the Spanish were aided by the Navajo and others. In 1699 a group of Navajo appeared in Spanish towns carrying French trophies and praising the French for their courage. The Spanish claimed there were French settlements on a large river thought to be the South Platte.

French trappers operated throughout the Nebraska region during the 1690s and 1700s, and many married Indian women. The Trapper's Bride, *by Miller, shows one such marriage.*

In 1720 Pedro de Villasur took a good-sized force from Santa Fe to drive out the French. On August 14, the Pawnee attacked them. Villasur and large numbers of his men were killed somewhere along the Platte, possibly near the site of North Platte or Columbus. In 1739 French brothers Paul and Pierre Mallet are said to have named a river the Platte (the name it still bears) and traveled along its banks for about twelve days. They crossed most of what is now Nebraska before turning southwest and finally arriving at Santa Fe.

When the English won the French and Indian War, the French gave up all their claims, leaving the Spanish in sole possession of all the vast lands west of the Mississippi. At the end of the American Revolution, lands of the United States reached as far west as the Mississippi, making a common frontier with Louisiana, the Spanish possession across the river. In 1801 Napoleon forced Spain to return all of Louisiana to France in the Treaty of Madrid. Two years later, in one of the most important and ingenious real estate deals in American history, the United States was able to buy Louisiana from France.

"THE MOST BEAUTIFUL I EVER BEHELD"

President Jefferson sent Meriwether Lewis and William Clark to explore the new land. Their party of about fifty men pushed up the Missouri. Clark wrote in his diary: "Arrived at the mouth of the great Platte River at 10 o'clock [on July 21, 1804]. This great river, being much more rapid than the Missouri, forces its current against the opposite shore. The current of this river comes with great velocity, rolling its sands in the Missouri, filling up its bed. . . . Captain Lewis and myself with six men in a pirogue went up this great river Platte about two miles . . . passing through different channels, none of them more than five or six feet deep. . . .

"I am told by one of our Party who wintered two winters on this river, that 'it is much wider above, and does not rise more than five or six feet,' spreds verry wide and . . . cannot be navigated with Boats or Perogues. The Indians pass this river in Skin Boats which is

The grave of the cruel Omaha chief, Blackbird, occupied a beautiful site above the Missouri River. Painting by George Catlin.

flat and will not turn over. The Otteaus (Oto) a small nation reside on the South Side 10 Leagues up, the Panies (Pawnee) on the Same Side 5 Leagues higher up.''

Among the interesting visits made by the explorers was one to the grave of malevolent Chief Blackbird, who had died four years before. On July 30, Captain Clark wrote, ''The most butifull prospect of the River up and Down the Countrey opposit presented it self which I ever beheld.'' The explorers sent out many invitations to the Indians to meet with them. On August 3, although most of the Indians were gone on their annual buffalo hunt, Lewis and Clark held a council with some of the Missouri and Oto at the Council Bluffs on the Nebraska side.

On August 18 a party sent to capture some deserters returned to camp with M.B. Reed, one of the deserters, and three Oto chiefs. Reed was tried and was "sentenced to run the Gantlet four times through the Party & that each man with 9 Swichies should punish him.... The three principal Chiefs petitioned for Pardin for this man. After we explained the injurey such men could doe them by false representations and explaning the customs of our Countrey they were all Satisifed with the propriety of the Sentence & was Witness to the punishment."

On September 7, Lewis and Clark made their last camp in Nebraska and went on up the Missouri. Just two years later, after one of the most successful explorations of all time, they returned.

MODEST BEGINNINGS

Almost on the heels of Lewis and Clark came trappers, traders, and soldiers. In 1805 trader, explorer, and merchant Manuel Lisa made the first of many trips up the Missouri in search of furs and other trade. In 1807 Lisa found the site of Bellevue. Manuel Lisa is sometimes known as the Father of Old Nebraska.

When Zebulon Pike went West in 1806, he held a grand council on the Republican River. More than four hundred Indians attended. Pike succeeded in making them lower the Spanish flag and raise the American. The exact location of this successful meeting has never been precisely determined. Kansas claims that it took place there, and Nebraskans are equally certain that it was in Nebraska. Regardless of the location, after Pike's journey Spanish authority in the area was broken.

In 1811 Wilson Price Hunt and his party went up the Missouri River on their way overland to establish Astoria in Oregon. The next year Robert Stuart led a party back from Astoria. On a very difficult journey they entered Nebraska, after spending the winter in Wyoming. They could not float down the shallow Platte in canoes, so they loaded their goods on an old horse bought from the Snake Indians. Finally they reached an island about 70 miles (113 kilometers) long, a landmark they recognized as Grand Island. At an Indian village nearby, they met some traders, traded their horse for a canoe, and floated down the Platte and the Missouri. Their travels resulted in valuable new knowledge about the Platte Valley.

On Manuel Lisa's annual trip up the Missouri in 1812, he established Fort Lisa, about ten miles (sixteen kilometers) north of Omaha. The first treaty between the United States and the Pawnee was negotiated in 1818. Fort Atkinson became the first European settlement in Nebraska, but it lasted only until 1827. When it was founded it was the most remote outpost of the United States. In 1823 Peter Sarpy established an American Fur Company post at Bellevue, south of Omaha. This proved to be the first permanent European settlement in what is now Nebraska.

The first wagon passed across the Nebraska region in 1824 with the William Ashley party. In the Treaty of Fort Atkinson, September 25, 1825, the Pawnee acknowledged the federal government. However, Nebraska had not been opened for settlement. The principal activity of non-Indians was trading with the Indians for furs.

Missionaries were the next group in Nebraska. The Baptist Missionary Union established a mission in 1833 at Bellevue to convert the Oto Indians. Moses Merrill preached Nebraska's first sermon that year. A Presbyterian mission was located there several years later.

Father Pierre Jean de Smet was the first Catholic missionary in the area, arriving in 1836. On a visit to the Oto village near Papillion, he was given a banquet by the first chief. The queen gave him a seat on a cushion "shining with grease." The meal consisted of a sort of stew and kind of pie. He did not want to offend the Indians by refusing, so he began to eat. The stew was made of buffalo tongue floating in a gravy of bear fat, thickened with wild sweet potato flour. Much to his surprise he found it excellent, and described with amusement the number of dogs that sat around watching every mouthful with envy.

Father de Smet traveled throughout almost the entire West in his many years of service, crossing Nebraska four times in all. He made seventeen passages up the Missouri River, water border of

Nebraska. The Pathfinder, John C. Frémont, also crossed Nebraska. Frémont and his guide, Kit Carson, carved their names in a rock on the bank of Rock Creek near Fairbury; but their monument can no longer be seen there.

WAGONS WESTWARD!

In the period that followed, Nebraska was important mainly as a highway to the West. A steady movement of pioneers flowed across the plains. The first major wave crossed Nebraska on the Oregon Trail.

Later, the Mormons were driven from their homes in Illinois, and in the winter of 1846-1847 more than six thousand of them camped

Mountain men of today make an annual covered-wagon pilgrimage to Fort Bridger on the Oregon Trail. The "Bridger Trek" honors Jim Bridger, who helped map the Oregon Trail and built the fort to make supplies available to the many covered-wagon trains on their way west in the 1800s.

in a temporary town known as Winter Quarters. It was built on both the Iowa and Nebraska sides of the Missouri River, near Council Bluffs, Iowa, and Omaha. In the spring the first Mormon pioneers started across Nebraska, followed by more and more over the ensuing years. The Oregon Trail and the Mormon Trail came together in Nebraska, although on opposite sides of the Platte River. The Oregon Trail followed much the same path blazed by the Stuart Astorian party more than thirty years before. The Mormon Trail followed the same route as Highway 30 across the state.

A journal writer on one of the wagon trains described the scene at one of the camps: "A singular spectacle. The hunters returning with the spoil; some erecting scaffolds, and others drying the meat. Of the women, some were washing, some ironing, some baking. At two of the tents the fiddle was employed in uttering its unaccustomed voice among the solitudes of the Platte; at one tent I heard singing; at others the occupants were engaged in reading, some the Bible, others poring over novels. While all this was going on that nothing might be wanting to complete the harmony of the scene a Campbellite preacher, named Foster, was reading a hymn, preparatory to religious worship. The fiddles were silenced, and those who had been occupied with that amusement, betook themselves to cards. Such is but a miniature of the great world we had left behind us, when we crossed the line that separates civilized man from the wilderness. But even here the variety of occupation, the active exercise of body and mind, either in labor or pleasure, the commingling of evil and good, show that the likeness is a true one."

The emigrants wrote messages on buffalo skulls and left them along the trail. The skulls bore the names of people of their party and instructions helpful to those who were coming later. Troublesome stream crossings were described; sites for pasturage and locations of wood were detailed.

The first Mormon party to cross the country used a novel method to keep track of how far they had traveled. William Clayton was assigned the task of counting each turn of the wheel. At the end of the day the distance was computed by multiplying the circumference of the wheel by the number of revolutions. Before the journey was

Bellevue, the first permanent European settlement in Nebraska. George Catlin.

over, however, Appleton Harmon designed a sort of pioneer "roadometer." Fortunately, it proved a great success, and Clayton was relieved of his counting duties.

The next great group of emigrants were those who came in 1849, straining every resource to reach California in time to make a strike in the gold fields. Crossing the Platte in 1849, "the line [of wagons] for two miles along the riverbank presented as busy an aspect as it ordinarily does in St. Louis, or any other small town in the States," according to one emigrant's journal.

"Four boats, each consisting of two dugouts fastened together, had been made by emigrants who had crossed before and gone on, others buying their rights and continuing the work. We paid $3 per wagon for the use of the boats, and swam the oxen. . . . Our 'boat' was called the *Two Pollies and Betsy,* from their being two dugouts, with a log between them. Joining forces with the twelve Cincinnati mule trains, the boat started off in style with 30 men to cordelle it against the current. The men were obliged to work in the water, which rendered it quite unpleasant; but by 4 o'clock we were across, and then drove the oxen down to swim.

"With all of our efforts, swimming and wading from that time until dark, we could only get three of them across; so had at last to let them return to the shore, and were obliged to keep watch of them until morning.... Again resumed our labors.... Fancy for one moment our feelings on observing the vast aggregation of oxen, mules, horses and wagons mixed indiscriminately with men, clothed, half-clad and even almost naked, encountering the elements that were temporarily stopping our progress....

"The onlookers witnessed sights ranging from the laughable to the alarming. In one place six men were assisted ashore by hanging to the tail of a mule, with a rider on him. A boat with a wagon containing women and children sank but was saved by striking a bar. I was carried by the swift current outside the jam of cattle, and saved myself by catching hold of the tail of an ox as I passed him, and letting him tow me to shore."

When the water was shallow enough, the teams were able to pull the wagons across the rivers.

NEBRASKA TERRITORY

The last great groups of pioneers in wagon trains came for many decades, in a seemingly endless stream. These were the settlers of Nebraska.

In 1844 an effort was made to have a territory of Nebraska created. But the move was defeated because those who favored slavery were alarmed by the prospect of a new free state. Ten years later, on May 30, 1854, Congress passed the Kansas-Nebraska Act proposed by Senator Stephen A. Douglas. This provided for what was supposed to become the slave state of Kansas and the free state of Nebraska.

President Franklin Pierce chose Francis Burt as first governor of the territory. But Burt died only two weeks after he arrived, and Thomas B. Cuming became acting governor. In 1855 the first legislature met at Omaha City, founded just the year before. Omaha served as the capital until 1867. The first census showed that 2,732 people lived in the territory; it was vastly larger than the present state of Nebraska, including Kansas and portions of the Dakotas, Colorado, Wyoming, and Montana.

After the territory was established, more settlers came in. There were a few slaves in Nebraska, but many settlers were opposed to slavery. The underground railroad, which smuggled slaves from the South up through the free states to safety in Canada, operated vigorously in Nebraska. John Brown, an active foe of slavery, brought many groups of black people from Kansas through Nebraska and on to freedom.

When the Civil War came, the territory was not well enough developed to play a large part. The First Regiment of Nebraska was enrolled on June 8, 1861. Altogether, 3,307 from Nebraska served in the Civil War, from a total population of only 30,000. Omaha and Pawnee Indians served in the army as scouts.

During the war, in 1862, the first Homestead Act was passed. This provided up to 160 acres (65 hectares) of land free to people who claimed it, lived on it for five years, and made certain improvements. Nebraska's Daniel Freeman applied for homestead land near Beatrice. The land office was not officially open until January 2,

1863, but Freeman was scheduled to leave for military service the night of January 1. By accident he met the young man who operated the land office and told him the story. The young man took Freeman to the office and allowed him to make his claim just after midnight. So Nebraska boasts that Freeman's application for homestead land was the first in the country.

After a would-be homesteader had found a suitable claim, his first step was to travel to the land office, often more than 100 miles (161 kilometers) away. If he were slow in filing, someone else might beat him and file a claim to the land he wanted. The *Beatrice Express* gave a graphic description of the Beatrice land office: "The jam was terrible, and the poor woman was obliged to beg for more room from fear of fainting. The applications poured in as fast as they could be taken care of all day, the crowd inside and out never growing smaller, for as fast as one applicant, with papers properly fixed up, would worm his way through the crowd to the door, and be cast out, panting and dripping with perspiration, another would squeeze in, and became part of the solid, surging mass within."

Many of those taking land in Nebraska were veterans of the Civil War who were looking for new frontiers after their release from service.

STATEHOOD

By 1864 the borders of Nebraska had been cut back almost to their present positions. In 1866 Congress passed a bill giving statehood to Nebraska. President Andrew Johnson vetoed the bill, but Congress passed it over the veto, and Nebraska became the nation's thirty-seventh state on March 1, 1867. David Butler was the first governor of the state.

The question of where to locate the state capital sparked many quarrels. Finally, the legislature appointed a special committee under Butler; it chose a spot in the middle of the prairie near a small village known as Lancaster. The committee's choice became Lincoln, the present capital of the state.

From 1854 until 1877, settlers had much trouble with the Indians, who were angry at being driven from their homes. There were many incidents such as the attack on a stagecoach shown here in a painting by George Simons.

Yesterday and Today

INDIAN WARS

As more and more covered wagons trundled across the prairie, the Indians watched with growing alarm from such historic spots as Sioux Lookout, southeast of North Platte. If the flood of settlers continued from the east, soon there would be no room left for the Indians on the hunting grounds that had so long been theirs.

From 1854 until 1877 there was almost constant trouble with the Indians across the plains, including Nebraska. There were many individual conflicts, but the one great cause was simply the fact that new settlers were driving native Americans from their homes.

Not all Indian battles were with the settlers. In 1873 a group of about three hundred Pawnee warriors and four hundred women were hunting under the supervision of the government agent. Spotting a plain filled with buffalo, they hurried over, to find that Sioux and Brule warriors had disguised themselves in buffalo robes. The Pawnee women hurried to a canyon, where they chanted the victory and death song. However, the Pawnee men were overpowered and were spared complete destruction only by the arrival of the cavalry. Bodies of sixty-five Pawnee were buried in one grave, and the Pawnee were never able to go on the hunt again.

In the 1870s the government began to move the Indians to Indian Territory in what is now Oklahoma. The Ponca refused to leave their homes. Taken by force, they were herded like animals across the plains under the troopers' guns. There were no roads, and the captives left a trail of red from sore and bleeding feet. Many fell sick. At Milford a tornado ripped their tents to shreds and destroyed their wagons.

The Ponca found their new home a land of hot and jagged rocks. Within a year, 158 of Chief Standing Bear's people died. Thirty of those who were left gathered their few possessions and started back to their old homes. After ten weeks of fighting to survive, they came to the land of the Omaha and were taken in by them. But the government ordered them back to Indian Territory.

Two lawyers, John L. Webster and Andrew J. Poppleton, heard of the Ponca's plight and took their plea to court. In one of the few cases of its kind, the Indians won, and the government was forced to permit them to stay in Nebraska. Their number has grown in recent years. The remainder of the tribe stayed on in Oklahoma.

None of the major battles that ended the Indian wars for all time was fought on Nebraska soil. However, one of the most dramatic events of the closing days of the war occurred at Fort Robinson. Thousands of Indians, led by their chiefs, were streaming to the fort to surrender and be placed on reservations. Many of them were following one of the great Indian chiefs—the famous Crazy Horse. At the last minute Crazy Horse refused to submit to capture. He was killed by one of the soldiers. The day of Indian mastery was over for all time.

The Cheyenne's bid for freedom is another great epic of the frontier. They had been sent to Indian Territory in 1877, but they escaped and made their way through Kansas and into Nebraska before they were captured and brought to Fort Robinson. The rest of the story was told by J. Greg Smith in *Outdoor Nebraska:* [The Cheyenne] "were imprisoned at the post for three months. On January 9 [1877] they made their second heroic bid for freedom. Using their few concealed guns, they opened fire on the soldiers guarding the barracks, overpowered them, and took their arms and ammunition. While the women and children fled across the river, eight warriors fought off the alarmed garrison. Many Cheyenne fell between the barracks and the river but most escaped to the buttes where the battle continued for two weeks in Warbonnet, Smiley, Hat Creek, and Sowbelly canyons.

"The Cheyenne Outbreak Battle is one of the ironies of the frontier. Many of the Cheyenne had been fighting for, not against, the army only two years before. General Crook considered them 'among the bravest and most efficient' of those who fought under him and Mackenzie against the Sioux in 1876 and '77."

Only one non-Indian, George Rawley, was killed in the Cheyenne's march across Nebraska. After the battles, the Cheyenne returned to the Red Cloud Indian Agency at Fort Robinson.

A GROWING STATE

In spite of the conflict with Indians during the period, the state continued to grow. The most important single reason was the coming of the railroad. One by one the ties were laid, beginning at Omaha. Slowly the tracks replaced the ruts of the old trails, as thousands of workers toiled under the watchful eye of troops protecting them from the Indians.

Fortunately for the early growth of Nebraska, the route of the great new railroad—the first to span the width of a continent—was laid across the heart of the state. The Union Pacific crossed Nebraska and hurried on to Utah to meet the Central Pacific from the West. Nebraska's part of the job was finished in 1867.

One of the railroad's first tasks was to transport cattle that had been driven up over the trails from Texas. Though Nebraska was not on the main Chisholm cattle trail, an extension led into the state. Schuyler was one of the first points on the Union Pacific from which great numbers of cattle were shipped. Ogallala was another important early shipping point for Texas cattle. After the cowboys had delivered their herds to the railroad towns, they usually looked for entertainment and ways to celebrate. Some of the Nebraska cattle towns were as rip-roaring as Dodge City.

From 1870 to 1890 the railroads did all they could to encourage settlers in Nebraska, knowing that the more people living there, the greater their business would be. As the number of farmers and small land claims increased, the cattle ranchers, with their great unfenced spreads, became increasingly disturbed. Intense rivalry developed between cattlemen and farmers. Fence wires were cut; there were killings on both sides; and constant cattle rustling decreased the ranchers' herds. When cases of disputed land ownership came to court, cattlemen were generally defeated by the homesteaders; there were usually more farmers on the juries than there were cattlemen.

Because they controlled the only practical means of marketing farm and ranch products, the railroads, in effect, enjoyed a monopoly. Both farmers and cattlemen complained about excessive rates and other unfair railroad practices.

A number of colorful events brightened the monotony of life on the frontier. One of these was the visit in 1872 of Grand Duke Alexis of Russia, who stopped at North Platte on his way to a buffalo hunt. The duke, twenty-two years old, was the brother of the Czar of Russia. To see that he got the greatest possible thrill from hunting America's biggest game, both General Phil Sheridan and Buffalo Bill Cody accompanied him. They made camp in the bend of Red Willow Creek, near the camp of Chief Spotted Tail of the Sioux. To entertain the royal visitor, the chief and his men staged a brilliant war dance.

Another distinguished visitor was the English Earl of Dunraven, who left Fort McPherson in 1874 with Buffalo Bill and one hundred warriors on a buffalo hunt of his own.

During the rush for gold in the Black Hills in 1876-1877, Sidney was the principal railroad stopping-point on the overland trek to the hills. As many as fifteen hundred gold seekers passed through Sidney in a day.

Nebraskans suffered their share of disasters. A grasshopper plague in 1874 drove countless settlers from the country in despair. The awful winter of 1880-1881 also took a heavy toll in Nebraska.

Those who think the Midwest is lacking in art and culture might find it surprising that America's first art association was founded at Lincoln in 1888.

The year 1890 brought the twin disasters of a drought and financial crash, and in 1891, eighteen thousand prairie schooners reversed the trend of pioneer days and trundled out of Nebraska.

Nebraska helped a rival prairie community celebrate in 1893 by organizing a thousand-mile (sixteen-hundred kilometer) horse race from Chadron to the Chicago World's Columbian Exposition. The race was won in the record time of thirteen days, sixteen hours. Nebraska held its own fair in 1898—the Trans-Mississippi International Exposition in Omaha. Heading the distinguished visitors was President William McKinley.

In 1904, the open range in Nebraska became history with the passage of the Kinkaid Law, which permitted homesteading of as much as 640 acres (260 hectares) per claim. One of Omaha's greatest tragedies occurred when the Easter tornado of 1913 caused loss of life and great damage.

A far greater disaster was World War I: 47,801 from Nebraska served, and 1,000 died.

The inspiring Nebraska capitol building was begun at Lincoln in 1922. A year later, as a remembrance of the past, one-hundred-year-old Chief Ruling-His-Sun at last was persuaded to sit down and smoke a peace pipe with his ancient enemies, the Sioux. The occasion was the fiftieth anniversary of the Battle of Massacre Canyon, which almost destroyed the Pawnee nation. Succeeding generations of both groups commemorate the event with an annual powwow and smoking of peace pipes.

In 1930, the Lincoln National Bank was the scene of one of the biggest bank robberies up to that time. About two million dollars was stolen from the vaults. In 1934, Nebraska made transportation history for the second time in a race to a Chicago world's fair. The Burlington *Zephyr* made the pioneer run from Omaha to the Century of Progess Exposition in record time and inaugurated the age of the streamlined diesel train.

The thirties was a period of mounting difficulties for the people of Nebraska. The Great Depression, which began in 1929, grew steadily worse; one of the worst droughts on record added further to the despair of farmers. Banks and insurance companies foreclosed on mortgages and took the property of hundreds of farmers. There were sporadic outbursts of violence. The situation began to ease when the drought let up and emergency measures (such as mortgage moratoriums) were taken to keep the farmers on their land.

During World War II, 120,000 men and women from Nebraska were in the armed services of the United States. Of these, 3,839 lost their lives. Historic old Fort Robinson was used as a war-dog training center during the war.

Omaha adopted a new city charter in 1957 and was named an all-American city. As the years went by, however, many sections of the city deteriorated. During the 1970s, the city began a massive rehabilitation program, with special attention to a dramatic new riverfront.

Also during the 1970s, Nebraska had the largest population increase of any midwestern state.

THE PEOPLE AND THEIR GOVERNMENT

The government of Nebraska is unique in the United States. Other state legislatures are divided into two houses, modeled on the national Congress. But Nebraska's legislature is made up of only one house. We call this a *unicameral* (one-house) legislature. The forty-three members of the Nebraska legislature are elected on a ballot that does not list them according to their party.

This unique system originated in 1914, when a report on the plan was drawn up and submitted by a committee whose secretary was Addison E. Sheldon. The report was debated for about twenty years. Finally, in 1934, the state constitution was amended by popular vote to provide for a unicameral legislature of not less than thirty nor more than fifty members. Those who advocated the plan claimed that it would be more economical, would eliminate passing the buck from one house to another, and would circumvent many of the roadblocks and delays of a two-house body.

The ethnic backgrounds of Nebraska people today are diverse. The first wave of immigrants from Europe came from Germany, and today there are more citizens of German background than any other in the state. Probably the next largest number are of Czech descent, followed by Swedish, Danish, Russian, English, Irish, and Polish.

About seven thousand American Indians now live in Nebraska. Many of their spokesmen say they are neglected and mistreated; long-delayed discussions and actions are being taken to improve their condition. The Winnebago and Omaha are the only groups now living on reservations in the state. Of the Pawnee—once the largest and most powerful group in the state—none remain.

Most of the Indians of Nebraska have adopted modern ways, but many old customs are still cherished. Each August the Ponca bring gifts to the Omaha in memory of the kindness shown them by the ancient Omaha people. The Winnebago keep up their annual

40

ceremonial dances at Winnebago in August, when they also celebrate other old customs, hold councils, and repeat ancient songs and legends. They practice their traditional handicrafts, making bracelets and rings, buckskin dresses and moccasins, bows and arrows, headdresses, and rugs.

Most of Nebraska's Indian children attend modern schools, but not many pursue higher education. Most of the younger generation wear modern clothing. Traditional Indian dress is seldom worn on the Omaha reservation, although beaded moccasins, bright shawls, and braided hair are not uncommon among the older women. Most of the Omaha are Christians. They attend church at the Pentecost of the Blackbird (Dutch Reformed) Church in Macy, one of the oldest places of worship in Nebraska.

The dead are remembered by feasts, prayers, and holy songs. Perhaps the most interesting tribute to the Omaha's historic past is the annual Powwow Council, held in August in an oak grove near Macy. More than a hundred tents are put in place around a permanent council lodge of bark. To the thump of drums, the tribe's symbolic dances are performed. Traditions, myths, and songs are part of the ceremonies. Much of the color and action of old Indian life is revived for a few days, and then the Omaha settle back into their usual lives as citizens of the space age.

The people of Nebraska are little more than a hundred years removed from their pioneer past, and many experiences of that period still influence life today. The firmness of character developed by confronting the awful loneliness, the grinding toil, and numerous dangers of the prairie must certainly have been passed on to many of the pioneers' descendants.

Pioneer women, especially, endured much. Mrs. N.M. Ayers, who settled in Furnas County as a bride in 1873, remembered some of her feelings fifty years later: "We traveled all day over vast prairies without seeing a tree or a shrub, not even a sage bush. I never longed to see a tree as I did that day. Our second day's drive brought us to Turkey Creek at noon and there for the first time since leaving Lowell we beheld the beautiful native trees for which we had been longing."

Pioneer life was usually begun in a dugout scooped from the side of a hill—cramped, dirty, and crawling with insects. If the claim had some timber, its settlers could build a log cabin. Most pioneer homes had to be built of "Nebraska marble," the tough, fibrous sod of the prairie. Blocks of sod 1 foot (.3 meter) wide and up to 1 yard (.9 meter) long were used. The sod blocks formed the walls, with dirt packed tightly between the blocks as mortar. Roofs were thatch or sod, supported on poles.

Those lucky enough to have wood used boards for the floor; others had to be content with the bare ground. In times of plentiful rain, the exterior of a sod house came to life. Waving grasses, blooming weeds, and riotous morning glories would appear, with even a prairie rose or two blushing on the wall.

Prairie fires were only one danger of pioneer life. Mrs. M.A. Freas recalled how a fire once swept down on her sod house in Furnas County: "We all ran for our lives and arrived safely on the plowed ground (about 80 rods [400 meters] from the house). The flames rolled on around us and left us safe. I said, 'Let us pray God in His mercy and goodness to save our little home.' We did pray. Some said God had nothing to do with it, but I will always believe He did for our home was saved, although the ground was burned black around it."

In April, 1893, the entire population (three thousand) of North Platte was threatened by an enormous prairie fire started by sparks from a railroad locomotive. Every able-bodied person fought the fire. Finally, after burning about thirty-five houses, it was turned away.

The grasshopper was another pioneer plague. The *Osceola Homesteader* wrote in 1874: "Our foreign readers must forgive us for giving so much grasshopper news. We really cannot help it. The air is filled with them, the ground is covered with them, and people think and talk of nothing else. It rains grasshoppers and snows grasshoppers. We cannot walk the streets without being struck in the face and eyes by grasshoppers, and we cannot sleep for dreaming grasshoppers, and if the little devils do not leave for some other clime soon, we shall go grasshopper crazy."

This early Nebraska sod and log cabin was typical of the type of home the pioneers had to build from the material available.

The conflict between Indians and new settlers was real and constant, but not all confrontations had tragic results. A favorite story on the frontier is retold by Fred Nelson in *Nebraskaland*. It concerned the "prairie wife who was surprised by 10 or 12 braves, probably Pawnee, as she was frying meat. The woman continued to cook as the Indians milled around the cabin, examining everything that caught their eyes. Some started to pilfer the cooked meat and the wife retaliated with a broom. She flew at the startled warriors like a skirted fury. The Indians practically took the door with them in their retreat from the broom-wielding demon. They did not return."

Most of the pioneers developed a fierce loyalty to Nebraska. But not all the settlers could take the life of the prairie, and some returned to their former homes. A traveler near Columbus went to a prairie house for a drink of water. He found a sign that read: "This claim for sale. Four miles to the nearest neighbor. Seven miles to the nearest schoolhouse. Fourteen miles to the nearest town. Two hundred feet to the nearest water. God bless our home! For further information address Thomas Ward, Oskaloosa, Iowa."

Natural Treasures

When Major Stephen H. Long passed Nebraska on his famous expedition of 1819, one of the members of his party wrote that the lands west of the Missouri were the "abode of perpetual desolation." This comment placed the great American desert on the map and gave much of the West an undeserved reputation for barrenness. The Union Pacific Railroad printed brochures to correct this impression of Nebraska. "What used to be the Great American Desert ... is actually the great national pasture ground.... The Platte will prove to be the northern Nile."

However, even today large numbers of non-Nebraskans have a mistaken impression of Nebraska. The state game commission points out, "Many outsiders regard Nebraska as a flat fertile plain that raises grain, cattle, an occasional dust storm, and little else."

What none of the early observers could guess from a casual look was that Nebraska had wonderfully fertile soil (probably its greatest single asset). What appeared to be dry earth was really almost "floating" on a sea of water. This "sea" consists of the largest supply of underground water in the nation. If all of it could be brought to the surface, it would cover the whole state to a depth of thirty-four feet (about ten meters). As supplies of fresh water dwindle, this vast reserve will certainly prove to be one of Nebraska's greatest sources of wealth.

Among other minerals, sand and gravel are available in almost limitless quantities. Nebraska produces many fine clays for bricks, ceramics, and other commercial uses. The Hastings clay is especially useful for brickmaking.

Known supplies of oil and natural gas have increased as explorations have pinpointed these invaluable resources.

In the early days, Nebraska was almost entirely a land without forest cover; today there are more than 1 million acres (404,686 hectares) of forest within the state. The native trees of the Nebraska

In the early days there were very few trees in Nebraska, but the people have planted so many that there are now forests in the state.

area were mostly cottonwoods and willows. Cottonwoods grew to great size there. Planted in 1871 by Mrs. Rhoda Simpson, the "King of the Cottonwoods" in Guide Rock reached nearly twenty-seven feet (eight meters) in circumference. Most of Nebraska's native trees were found along the streams. One of the finest stands of hardwood timber in the country grows in Ponca State Park.

Nebraskans planted as many trees as they could. In 1860 William Stolley planted six thousand trees, and this small forest is now the basis of Stolley State Park. Nebraska's eminent botanist Dr. Charles Bessey had a dream that forests would grow in Nebraska, even though nature had not provided them. In 1902 he persuaded President Theodore Roosevelt to establish the Nebraska National Forest. The plan was to demonstrate that forests could be planted on the Great Plains and to test the best kinds of trees for such an area. Today the Nebraska National Forest encompasses thousands of acres.

After the drought of the mid-1930s, shelter belts were planted across the plains. These check wind erosion and furnish timber.

Tall prairie grasses flourish in the eastern region; short, nourishing grasses grow in the western portion of Nebraska. The flowers and plants that grow in these two grass regions are very different. In the drier, low-grass region, cactus and other semiarid regional plants are found. However, the western tablelands are a riot of blossom in springtime when there have been good rains. Even in the Badlands and Brule Clay regions, there are flowers such as yellow umbels. In various parts of the state, wild flowers are abundant; one of the more spectacular is Frémont's primrose, with blossoms almost two inches (five centimeters) in diameter. Wild rose, phlox, violet, spiderwort, yellow lady's slipper, columbine, water lily, petunia, anemone, goldenrod, and sunflower are found, along with many others.

The abundant grasses and groves of trees nourished by Nebraska's waterways provide food and shelter for a surprising collection of animals and birds.

Most spectacular, of course, were the buffalo, which have long since vanished, except for a few herds raised by individuals or the state. Millions of these huge beasts once roamed the prairies.

46

Wild flowers are abundant in various parts of Nebraska. These sunflowers were photographed near Gavins Point Dam on the South Dakota-Nebraska border.

Most of the buffalo were exterminated by hunters over a short period of years. The meat was used by railroad workers and also helped many pioneers to exist; the skins were in great demand for robes. Of course, overhunting also caused great waste. However, it would not have been possible for the buffalo to survive even if they had not been hunted. The coming of farming, fences, and other advances of civilization would have destroyed their habitat and food sources in any event.

Some authorities feel that at one time elk may have been even more abundant than buffalo in Nebraska; however, there are no records to prove this claim. Mule deer, white-tail deer, and pronghorn antelope were other once-numerous native plains animals. Today only the smaller animals are found in any numbers.

More than four hundred species of birds have been known in Nebraska. These range from the slender sandhill crane to the plump wild turkey. The native wild turkeys were killed off, but twenty-eight were brought to Nebraska from other states in 1959, and now they are estimated at several thousand. Other popular game birds are quail, prairie chicken, and the hooded merganser duck.

An immigrant to Nebraska is probably the most numerous and popular of all the state's birds. In 1915 a few pheasants were imported from China. Nebraska's pheasant population today is estimated in multimillion figures.

People Use Their Treasures

CATTLE AND CROPS

Marching head to tail in one long, plodding line, the cattle in Nebraska would stretch twice across the United States. In the 1960s Omaha replaced Chicago as the world's largest livestock market.

Nebraska ranks third among all states in total annual production of livestock and poultry. The state produces seven million head of what Nebraskans claim is the best beef in the world. As early as 1817, English naturalist John Bradbury thought the plains, then considered useless, might someday prove valuable. He would probably be pleased to know how true his prediction was.

That same land produces crops worth nearly three billion dollars—ranking third in rye and sorghum grain, fourth in winter wheat, and fifth in corn. Total agricultural income of the state is more than four billion dollars. More than 3 million acres (1.2 million hectares) of Nebraska farmland are irrigated.

MANUFACTURING, MINING, AND MINERALS

The value of agricultural production is still considerably more than that of manufacturing in Nebraska, but industry has grown rapidly in the state. Total value of manufacturing in Nebraska comes to nearly two billion dollars per year.

Much of the state's manufacturing is based on agriculture. Omaha is the largest meat-packing and processing center in the United States, having won the title from its one-time rival, Chicago.

Omaha usually is considered one of the largest food processing centers in the world. The state's processed foods include canned fruits and vegetables, flour, soft drinks, malt liquors, candy, butter, cheese and ice cream, feeds for livestock and poultry, sugar, coffee,

As the sun goes down, this Nebraska cowboy's duties are over for the day.

animal and vegetable fats and oils, spaghetti, noodles, macaroni, cereals, vinegar, gelatin, powdered milk, potato chips, and salad dressings. Omaha is one of the largest centers for processing frozen foods.

Dawson County is the nation's number one hay processor, much of it processed alfalfa. Like almost everything else, the alfalfa industry has been revolutionized. Instead of haystacks, "dehy" (dehydrating) plants line the roadsides. Trucks roll in with the green alfalfa directly from the fields. Six- to eight-ton (5.4 to 7.2 metric tons) loads of fresh-cut hay are digested in one gulp of a great chopper. The hay flows through grinders, bins, jets of air, furnaces, and mills of several kinds. When it comes out after a thirty-minute trip through a raging furnace, it is in the form of green pellets of nutritious alfalfa hay—"green gold." Bagged or in bulk, alfalfa pellets are year-round high-protein feed for the nation's livestock.

Nebraska's yearly production of dehydrated alfalfa equals nearly half the nation's total. The bulk of Nebraska's annual production of alfalfa finds its way into the state's eighty-two dehydrating plants. Each plant has as many as a half dozen drums. Of the total drums in the United States, nearly half are in Nebraska. Of these, Dawson County alone has more than sixty. At night the glowing cylinders of the furnace drums and the luminous smoke are bright beacons along the highway.

Other manufactured products include automobile parts and accessories, bedding, medicines, electrical machinery, communication equipment, air-conditioners, furniture, store fixtures, window shades and blinds, footwear, leather goods, millwork, tools, hardware, culverts, pipe, fencing, frozen-food lockers, grain bins, truck trailers, oil burners, farm equipment, wire, paper bags, roof materials, brick, tile, mirrors, monuments, glass cloth, cigars, boats, scooters, trailers, brooms, brushes, jewelry, toys, athletic goods, bakery supplies, and refined metals.

Omaha has been a leading center of lead smelting. Nebraska ranks among the low group of petroleum-producing states. Natural gas is also produced. However, production of both oil and natural gas is declining. Limestone is quarried in southeastern Nebraska for use as

This combine is gathering wheat from one of Nebraska's many wheat farms.

cut stone in buildings, in cement, and as fertilizer. Sand and gravel, pumice, clay, and gem stones are also produced. Mineral production in Nebraska totals about 100 million dollars.

TRANSPORTATION AND COMMUNICATION

In 1865 General W.T. Sherman, fresh from his triumphs in Georgia in the Civil War, was on hand in Nebraska to help the territory celebrate the completion of its first miles of railroad. The general and twenty other distinguished guests rode on a flatcar along the new rail line from Omaha to Salings' Grove. They sat on nail kegs—the only available seats.

Nebraska land was first broken for railroads in 1863; the first rails were laid two years later. During 1866, 250 miles (400 kilometers) of railroad were laid, and in 1867 the final 240 miles (384 kilometers) across the state were finished. By 1869, Nebraska was on the main line of rail travel across the country. The first permanent railroad bridge was built over the Missouri River between Omaha and Council Bluffs in 1872.

There was great peril for early rail travelers across the prairies. Flimsy bridges could collapse at any time under the weight of a train. Whenever a locomotive gained any speed, it was in grave danger of jumping the tracks; sparks frequently set the wooden cars on fire, and bandits frequently held up trains, robbed passengers, and stole valuable cargo.

Today, Omaha is the fourth largest rail center in the United States and is still the general headquarters for the Union Pacific Railroad, the transcontinental rail pioneer.

The first steamboat to travel on the Missouri was the *Western Engineer* in 1819. Under the command of Major Stephen H. Long, it puffed as far north as Fort Lisa, above Omaha.

By 1830 the American Fur Company had launched a fleet of shallow-draft steamboats on the Missouri. There were the *Yellowstone, Omega, Assiniboin,* and *Nimrod.* By 1857 fifty steamboats ran on the Missouri as far north as Omaha. At the height of the Missouri steamboat period, in 1859, 268 boats were touching at Omaha. Brownville also starred as a river port.

As the railroads took away business, it seemed that Missouri River transportation was becoming a thing of the past. Today a 9-foot (2.7-meter) channel dredged in the Missouri makes Omaha a port once again. Barges propelled by busy towboats are bringing an increasing amount of freight up the river.

For "fast" and "dependable" transportation in the early days, the stagecoach was the thing. Famed stage line owner Ben Holladay operated a daily stage across Nebraska over the Oregon Trail as early as 1861. Holladay broke the record for overland travel by stage, thundering between Salt Lake City, Utah, and Atchison, Kansas, at an average speed of 160 miles (257 kilometers) per day and a cost of ten dollars per mile. In 1866 Wells Fargo bought the Holladay company. Stagecoaches were still carrying passengers and freight in the Nebraska back country as late as 1900.

An interesting experiment in overland transportation was the great "steam wagon" made for Major J.R. Brown. With its wheels churning the dirt, its smokestack belching clouds of smoke, the steam wagon made an impressive start as it lumbered out of Nebraska City in 1862, hauling ten wagons and 35 tons (31.75 metric tons) of freight over the prairie. It lasted for eight miles (nearly thirteen kilometers), broke down, and never moved again under its own steam.

Today Nebraska boasts a network of interstate and other highways, many of them converging at Omaha. The Platte Valley Park-

The busy towboat Sioux City *propels a huge barge in the Missouri River at Omaha.*

*In the early days, communications in Nebraska depended on
the Pony Express, the fastest mail carrier of the times.*

way, a leading modern interstate highway, is dotted with ponds and
lakes. This man-made chain of lakes is a unique major recreation
feature.

Omaha today is served by major truck lines, railroads, and airlines.
By air the city is 2½ hours from New York and 3 hours from Los
Angeles.

Nebraska had the advantage of one of the most famous means of
communication in history—the Pony Express, fastest mail carrier of
its time. Its brief moment of glory ended with the arrival of the
telegraph. The August, 1860, issue of the *New York Times* noted that
telegraph lines had reached "westward to the half-peopled wilds of
Nebraska." When the line reached Brownville, the territory sent its
greetings to the other states. Nebraska's first telephone line was
installed between Omaha and Council Bluffs, Iowa, in 1877.

The state's earliest newspaper was the *Nebraska Palladium and
Platte Valley Advocate,* established at Bellevue in 1854. A novel early
newspaper was the *Pioneer on Wheels,* so named because it was
printed in a boxcar at North Platte. The most prominent newspaper
of the state is the *Omaha World-Herald.* This distinguished journal
gained particular notice when William Jennings Bryan became its
editor in 1894.

Human Treasures

THE GREAT COMMONER

William Jennings Bryan was not a native of Nebraska, but for the largest part of his spectacular political career he was associated with the state. After moving to Lincoln in 1887, he began a law practice. Bryan was elected to Congress from Nebraska in 1890, the first Democratic congressman from the state.

He soon became widely recognized for his gifts as an eloquent speaker, and he was later considered one of America's greatest orators.

Bryan joined the Chautauqua lecture circuit and in a few years was known throughout the country. He promoted what was known as the free coinage of silver. His most famous speech opposed the gold standard and was called the "Cross of Gold" speech. By the time of the Democratic national convention in 1896, he had become so prominent that he was the party's nominee for the presidency. Bryan was defeated by McKinley, but he remained the key leader of the Democratic party until 1912.

In 1900 he again ran for president and was defeated by McKinley and Theodore Roosevelt. In 1901 he founded a weekly paper, *The Commoner,* to carry on his fight against the wealthy and powerful people he felt controlled American politics. After a round-the-world tour in 1905 and 1906, he ran for president in 1908 and was again defeated, this time by William Howard Taft.

Bryan did not run for the presidency in 1912, but he was influential in nominating Woodrow Wilson. Bryan became Wilson's secretary of state and served in that post until 1915.

Bryan's last appearance in the world spotlight was a strange one. A Tennessee teacher, John T. Scopes, had been arrested for teaching evolution in violation of a local law. Famous attorney Clarence Darrow defended Scopes. William Jennings Bryan was the principal attorney for the prosecution. Bryan won the Scopes trial, one of the most famous in history. But he died a few days after its close and was buried at Arlington National Cemetery.

GEORGE WILLIAM NORRIS

Another famous political figure, George William Norris, was a Nebraskan by adoption. He moved to Beaver City, Nebraska, in 1885 and became prosecuting attorney of Furnas County. He served his first term as a Republican congressman from Nebraska and was elected to the Senate in 1913. Nebraska returned him to office for five straight terms. He served the state for a total of forty-seven years in Congress. Although he was elected as a Republican, for much of his period in office he considered himself an independent. Unafraid of party powers, he believed he owed explanations to no one but the voters who elected him.

A friend, J.E. Lawrence, wrote of Norris: "Virtually alone in the early 20's in one of the most conservative eras of American history, he carried on the discouraging battle which led to the ultimate establishment of the Tennessee Valley Authority. That victory established a sound, inspiring pattern for the conservation of natural resources, which has withstood a hundred powerful attacks. Twelve years of congressional battle went into it." One of the great dams of the Tennessee Valley, Norris Dam, near Knoxville, was named in his honor.

Norris opposed the United States' entry into World War I, but he supported the country's part in World War II. Among his important legislation were the Norris-La Guardia Anti-injunction Act and the Lame Duck Amendment to the United States Constitution in 1933.

In Nebraska, Senator Norris has been called the greatest influence in the creation of the state's unicameral legislature. He also was responsible for a series of dams for power and conservation in the Platte Valley. This project has come to be known as the Little TVA.

Profiles in Courage, by President John Kennedy, includes Senator Norris as an example of an American who stood by his beliefs despite great danger to his career. At the age of eighty-one, George W. Norris was defeated for re-election, his first defeat in forty-seven years in public office. He returned to his home at McCook and spent his final years writing his autobiography, *The Fighting Liberal.* He finished the book just eight weeks before his death in 1944.

OTHER PUBLIC FIGURES

In addition to his work for Arbor Day, Julius Sterling Morton made many other contributions to his nation and to his adopted state. In 1858 he became secretary of the Nebraska Territory and then acting governor. In 1893 President Grover Cleveland, at the start of his second term, appointed Morton secretary of agriculture. He became the first person from Nebraska to serve on a president's cabinet.

Morton's oldest son, Joy, was the founder of the Morton Salt Company. Also a tree-lover, Joy Morton established Morton Arboretum, near Chicago, one of the finest and most complete collections of trees and shrubs in the world.

Julius Sterling Morton's second son, Paul, became secretary of the navy under President Theodore Roosevelt; he was also president of the Equitable Life Assurance Company.

In 1923 the Morton sons gave the Morton estate at Nebraska City, including the fifty-two-room Arbor Lodge, to the state. It is now Arbor Lodge State Historical Park.

Arbor Lodge (below) is now part of Arbor Lodge State Historical Park.

David Butler has been called the "foremost figure in early state politics." In 1871 he was impeached and removed from the office of governor, charged with illegal use of state school money. He later paid back all the funds he was accused of taking, and in 1882 the people of his district showed their confidence in him by electing him a state senator.

One of the most enduring of the state's political leaders was Tom Dennison, labeled Omaha's "boss" from about the beginning of the century until his death in 1934. It was said that he began his career as a gambler and got into politics to protect his gambling interests.

This United States postage stamp honors Willa Cather, the famous Nebraska author who won a Pulitzer Prize for her novel, One of Ours.

Perhaps one of the most famous politicians to be associated with Nebraska in recent times is Gerald R. Ford. He was born in Omaha in 1913. Ford served as vice president of the United States in 1973-74 and president from August 9, 1974, to January 20, 1977.

Walter Judd, native of Rising City, served as a medical missionary in China, becoming a leading authority on the Far East. He was elected to the House of Representatives from Minnesota for ten consecutive terms.

Charles G. Dawes, vice president of the United States and sponsor of the Dawes Plan, had law offices in Lincoln in the same building as William Jennings Bryan. During the same period in which Bryan and Dawes lived in Lincoln, one of America's best-known military men, General John J. Pershing, served on the staff of the University of Nebraska as a military science instructor.

One of the largest fortunes gained in Nebraska was that of George A. Joslyn of Omaha, whose wealth came from the operation of a newspaper cooperative service—The Western Newspaper Union. The Joslyn family gave the Joslyn Museum at Omaha to the city in memory of the family founder.

In the field of scholarship, law authority Dean Roscoe Pound has been called the "most learned man produced in the state." Another outstanding scientist and educator is George W. Beadle, former president of the University of Chicago, who was born near Wahoo.

CREATIVE NEBRASKANS

A number of American writers have been associated with Nebraska.

The parents of Willa Cather brought her to Red Cloud at the age of nine. Her writings not only gave her fame but promoted understanding of the prairie region where she made her home. Her book *O Pioneers,* published in 1913, marked the beginning of a long period of interest in literature about Nebraska. This book has been called a "memorable example of the modern regional novel." In 1923 Willa Cather was awarded the Pulitzer Prize for her novel *One of Ours.* One of her best-known works was *Death Comes for the Archbishop,* published in 1927.

Mari Sandoz grew up in Nebraska's Sandhills country. Her father, Jules Sandoz, came from Switzerland to be a Sandhills pioneer. Mari Sandoz's best-known book is *Old Jules,* based on the life of her father. For this she won the Atlantic Monthly Prize.

Novelist Bess Streeter Aldrich was another who liked to write about pioneer life on the prairies. *A Lantern in Her Hand* includes the true story of Hangman's Tree near Murray. One of the best-known and most skillful mystery-story writers from Nebraska is Mignon Good Eberhart.

Nebraska poet John Gneisenau Neihardt spent thirty years on *The Cycle of the West,* a five-"song" volume of epic poetry. Well-known names of the Old West charge through the work. Neihardt graduated from Nebraska Normal College (Wayne State) at the age of sixteen. He spent much time with Omaha Indians and added to his store of western lore. In 1921 he was named poet laureate of Nebraska by the legislature. This was the first time any state had ever made such an appointment. Neihardt became known as the Poet of the West.

Edwin Ford Piper is another of Nebraska's better-known poets. His *Barbed Wire and Other Poems* told of the disappearance of the free cattle range.

Dr. Richard Tanner of Norfolk was an early plainsman who came to be known as Diamond Dick. His adventures were fictionalized in the popular *Diamond Dick* novels that delighted so many young people of an earlier day.

Art in Nebraska has ranged from murals drawn by Indians on tepee walls to the most modern works of highly trained artists.

Suzette La Flesche Tibbles, a part-Indian artist of the prominent La Flesche family, was born at Bellevue in 1854. She created many paintings and illustrated a book printed in 1898—*Oo-Mah-Ha Ta-Wa-Tha.* The drawings for this book are thought to be the first work by an Indian artist ever published. Charles S. Simmons of Scottsbluff gained a reputation as a painter of frontier scenes.

One of America's most distinguished composers and conductors, Howard Hanson, was a native of Nebraska.

Some of the boys from Father Flanagan's Boys Town, the internationally known institution that houses, educates, and trains homeless or underpriviledged boys.

SUCH INTERESTING PEOPLE

In 1917 an Omaha priest borrowed ninety dollars from a friend and began a career that made him "an international symbol of spiritual and material hope for millions." The priest was the Right Reverend Monsignor Edward J. Flanagan, who became known all over the world as Father Flanagan.

Father Flanagan used the ninety dollars for the first month's rent on an old house in Omaha. To this house he brought a growing number of homeless boys. The first Christmas after the home was opened, the dinner consisted of a barrel of sauerkraut donated by a friend. Father Flanagan kept up the work, supported by gifts, until the home was so crowded it was moved to the old German Civic Center.

Finally, Father Flanagan acquired land near Omaha and moved his boys into temporary wooden barracks. Today Boys Town, with a staff of trained and experienced workers, has grown considerably. It has high schools and grade schools, substantial dormitories for grade-school boys, and cottage houses for high-school boys. It provides every facility for training and rehabilitating needy boys. The "alumni" of Boys Town now number many thousands.

Father Flanagan spent much time in his later years advising and counseling organizations around the world on how to deal with homeless or delinquent young people. He died in Germany in 1948.

William F. (Buffalo Bill) Cody has been associated with many states. He was already famous when he came to North Platte in 1870 to make his home. He was the most famous citizen of North Platte for almost thirty years. Scouts Rest was the name of his ranch located northwest of the town. There he organized and rehearsed his world-traveling Wild West Show in 1883. The show was performed for kings and queens, as well as everyday people throughout the world.

In the tradition of Buffalo Bill, Nebraskan Jim Houston became the world's champion bronco rider in 1965.

The unselfishness of Samuel Allis deserves to be remembered. He had been robbed by the Indians at a time when he was "in distress and in a state of starvation." Later, when the Indians were suffering terribly from smallpox, Samuel Allis forgot his former mistreatment and vaccinated more than two thousand of the Pawnee tribe. The story has an unusual ending. When the Pawnee received a grant to pay for a tract of land, they insisted that Samuel Allis be given a thousand dollars because they "felt that he should be paid for these things."

An Omaha man who "gained several fortunes" and even greater fame as an eccentric was George F. Train. As an independent he ran for president of the United States in 1872. He also published a newspaper in New York, and was jailed for printing certain passages from the Bible that the courts said were obscene.

Nebraska boasts an unusual number of well-known entertainers. These include Harold Lloyd, Fred Astaire, Henry Fonda, Marlon Brando, Robert Taylor, and Dick Cavett.

The modest fame of Fred Patzel of Norfolk is still remembered by some Nebraskans. In 1926 Fred won the national hog-calling contest and was asked to demonstrate his skill over the local Norfolk radio station. His prize-winning bellow put the station off the air.

Teaching and Learning

The largest institution of higher education in the state is the University of Nebraska in Lincoln. The Nebraska legislature provided for a state university in an act of February 16, 1869. The first building was completed at Lincoln in 1871.

Today the university enrolls more than thirty thousand and has branches in many parts of the state. The university operates the Nebraska Center for Continuing Education, housed in a striking structure designed to accommodate educational seminars and conferences. Each year hundreds of meetings of distinguished scientists, educators, and other authorities are conducted at the center.

Other universities and colleges at Lincoln include Nebraska Wesleyan University, a Methodist institution, and Union College, sponsored by the Seventh Day Adventists.

Edward and John Creighton came to Omaha in 1856 and built a large fortune on the operation of the Western Union Telegraph Company. In 1876 Mary Lucretia Creighton, widow of Edward, left $100,000 to found a school in memory of her husband. Over the years, John A. Creighton provided more than two million dollars for Creighton University. About a year after the school was founded, the Jesuits were given control.

State institutions in addition to the university are Chadron State College, Kearney State College, Peru State College, and Wayne State College. Other institutions of higher education include Midland Lutheran College of Fremont; Concordia Teachers College, Seward; and Dana College, Blair—all Lutheran four-year colleges. Hastings College is Presbyterian.

Nebraska's first school was set up at Fort Atkinson in 1820. Missionaries soon established schools for the Indians. The first school for non-Indian children outside of the fort was begun at Bellevue in 1849. As time went by and the scattered population could afford to do so, schools were set up in various localities.

The territory's first legislature passed a law authorizing school districts, administered by school boards, to establish free elementary schools. Free high schools were not provided until 1875.

Enchantment of Nebraska

PATHWAY TO THE GOLDEN WEST

For more than a century the wide Platte Valley has been the high-road to the American West. But Nebraska is more than a mere pathway. Here is a land where the West that was wild continues to mingle with evidences of the most modern civilization.

Giant cattle herds still roam the unfenced prairies of a hundred years ago. But nuclear reactors power modern industry, and superhighways lace the green countryside, replacing the ruts of the Oregon Trail. Up-to-date cities have grown from the tracks of the Mormon wagons, and yet some of these are the sites of Indian pow-wows and celebrations.

For the visitor there are the joys of farm and ranch vacations and many fine state parks with fantastic scenery. The state abounds with historical restorations and reproductions, as well as some of the finest museums, music, and other cultural attractions anywhere.

LINCOLN, AN ARCHITECTURAL WONDER

"I came expecting to find a barren plain with possibly a few trees and modern buildings, and instead I found one of the architectural wonders of the world," wrote a foreign visitor to Lincoln. He was referring to the state capitol building, which authority Linus Burr Smith declared was "world famous as an architectural triumph."

In 1948, five hundred of the country's leading architects were polled to determine the twenty-five finest buildings the world has ever seen. When the results were made known, the Nebraska capitol ranked fourth.

Nebraska has had five capitol buildings—two territorial capitols in Omaha and three state capitols in Lincoln. The design for the present building was chosen in 1920 by a panel of jurors who considered the

Opposite: The beautiful Nebraska state capitol
at Lincoln was designed by Bertram Grosvenor Goodhue.

entries by number without knowing any of the architects' names. The winning design was the work of Bertram Grosvenor Goodhue.

According to Jane Tenhulzen: "Goodhue designed the beautiful ten-million-dollar State House as an expression of the Nebraska pioneer faith and frontier hope. Its tower rises as an exclamation point over a broad, firm base in daring defiance of the tradition that capitols should have pillars and domes. It stands as a crow's nest on a ship, surveying the rippling prairie, its golden tip symbolizing the inherent purpose of its citizens."

Ground was broken for the building in 1922; the new capitol grew up around the old, which was still being used. Nebraska maintained its reputation for thrift by building the new capitol only as funds became available. When it was completed and dedicated in 1932, it was completely paid for—even though it was finished in the heart of the depression and drought years.

The *New York Times* commented: "Either it will be a building of impressive force that will stretch its power milleniums in the future or it will be a stern-browed reminder of the money that could have been spent in better ways. Certainly, it will be no nonentity—no timid copy of dead art. Nebraska has been brave—has dared—where other states have bought their capitols more or less ready-to-wear, of the standardized Washington model."

The years have seemed to judge the capitol an unqualified success. The visitor today sees the massive building with the lofty limestone pinnacle stretching boldly against the prairie sky to a height of 400 feet (120 meters)—"a monument of the past and a promise of the future."

The symbolism of the carvings, murals, mosaics, and other art is so rich that their full meaning is difficult to grasp in only one visit. "Gifts of nature" is the theme for the floor, walls, and ceiling of the vestibule. The mosaics required years of painstaking effort, cutting, fitting, and placing. Hildreth Meirie was the tile designer, and it is said she considered the capitol mosaics her greatest work.

The rotunda art, in the very heart of the building, represents "creative energies." Dominating the rotunda floor is a giant mosaic of Ceres, goddess of agriculture. High above the floor is the dome of the rotunda, bearing the figures of Charity, Faith, Courage, Temperance, Wisdom, Justice, and Magnanimity. The viewer's eye is held by the great rotunda chandelier, the largest of its kind in the world, a huge bronze creation of 136 lights, suspended on a chain designed to hold 6,000 pounds (2,700 kilograms). High above, the rotunda is encircled by twenty-four columns of the finest French marble, noted for its regular veining and soft glow. The rotunda balcony is guarded by a magnificently carved railing of onyx, featuring sculptured meadowlark and buffalo.

The murals in the hall and the rotunda are the work of two artists. The homesteader's series was made by James Penney, with lavish use of reds, yellows, browns, buffs, and other typical Nebraska colors. Inside the rotunda, the three heroic murals painted by Kenneth Evett represent the work of the head, hands, and heart.

West of the great rotunda, lawmakers meet in the unicameral legislative chamber. Since Nebraska is the only state with a single legislative house, its capitol is the only one with a single legislative chamber.

Many of the capitol's interior rooms show the loving care of artists and craftsmen. The ceiling in the Supreme Court is a remarkable example. The wood used is American walnut, and there are nearly eight thousand separate pieces glued and pegged together, using no nails.

The outside of the capitol is noteworthy for its many carvings, bas-reliefs, sculptures, and inscriptions. One of the finest is a relief panel in the south balcony showing Franklin, Washington, and other leaders. Columns of the south entrance are topped by figures of lawmakers of ancient lands. Nebraska history is the theme of panels on the northeast corner. Heroic figures guard the lower bases of the tower. Most of the capitol's stone relief work was done by Lee Lawrie.

Above all looms the gold-glazed tower, topped by the gigantic statue of the Sower—a symbolic figure "sowing the seeds of good will for a more noble living in the future." The statue is a bronze shell almost 1 inch (2.5 centimeters) thick, about 19 feet (5.7 meters) high on a base 13 feet (3.9 meters) high. Figure and base together weigh about 9 tons (8 metric tons).

Watching over the west steps is one of the nation's most impressive pieces of sculpture—the statue of Abraham Lincoln by Daniel Chester French, who did the Lincoln statue in the Lincoln Memoral at Washington.

When the documents and furniture of the state government were moved from Omaha to Lincoln in 1868, there were only thirty people living in the new capital. The move was made at night to escape the armed bands of Omaha boosters, who were determined to keep the capital by force if necessary. Only a year later Lincoln's population had risen to five hundred, and by 1870 it had reached twenty-five hundred. Today Lincoln is Nebraska's second largest city.

Another of Lincoln's notable state buildings is the regal and elegant executive mansion, completed in 1957. Its striking rooms

The governor's mansion at Lincoln.

include the emerald state drawing room, enhanced by the elegance of hand-cut crystal chandeliers. Commuting is no problem for the governor, since the mansion lies almost within the shadow of the capitol.

The University of Nebraska is a leader in Lincoln's cultural affairs. The Nebraska State Museum is housed in Morrill Hall on the university campus. One of the most important exhibits is that of the world's largest mammoth, housed in Elephant Hall. Ralph Mueller Planetarium is also connected with the museum. Among the best-known landmarks on the campus is the Memorial Stadium, where many outstanding games have been played.

The university is also the home of one of the finest small art galleries in the country. The gallery was a gift of the Sheldon family in memory of Mary Frances Sheldon and her brother, A. Bromley Sheldon. The family wanted to provide the university with a worthy building to house its extensive art collections. Jim Forrest has said, "the gallery is both a building to house beauty and a thing of beauty in itself." Philip Johnson of New York was the architect, and he wrote: "Never have I known such joy in working out a problem. . . . I am astonished at the artistic sophistication, at the direct, straightforward interest in the arts, so refreshing after the status-seeking snobbishness of many East Coast art lovers."

Another outstanding cultural institution housed at the university is the Nebraska State Historical Society.

Of the buildings owned by the city, one of the most impressive is Pershing Municipal Auditorium. In a matter of hours the seven-thousand-seat auditorium can become a boxing or wrestling arena, a roller skating rink, exhibition hall, or circus arena. Over the main entrance is the largest ceramic mosaic tile mural ever executed in the United States; it shows the many activities possible inside.

Music lovers can enjoy numerous musical attractions, both imported and local, highlighted by the Lincoln Symphony Orchestra.

The Lincoln home of William Jennings Bryan is open to the public as a registered national historic landmark. Here the national leader made his home until 1917. The first floor has been restored with the original furnishings and memorabilia of the Bryans.

A recreation center for Lincoln is Antelope Park. Its children's zoo is considered one of the outstanding in the nation. Also a delight for children is the Iron Horse Railroad, a scale replica of the famous C.P. Huntington locomotive. Hordes of happy young passengers ride around its ½-mile track (.8 kilometer), which winds along a creek, across a trestle, and through a tunnel. Across from Antelope Park, visitors enjoy the majestic beauty of the Sunken Gardens. Scene of many productions under the stars is Pinewood Bowl, set deep in Pioneer Park.

DOORMAN OF THE WESTERN GATE: OMAHA

On June 24, 1854, the Omaha Indians signed a treaty giving up their age-old homelands. There a great city, named after them, was destined to grow. To celebrate, a group of people crossed the Missouri River on the ferry from Council Bluffs, Iowa, for a Fourth of July celebration and picnic on what is now Capitol Hill. A toast to Nebraska was offered, and Hadley D. Johnson replied with a "salute" from an anvil cannon. The hole in the top of the anvil was filled with powder, and a fuse was put in. When the fuse was lighted, the anvil flew a hundred feet (thirty meters) into the air with a mighty roar. A group of Indians hurried over to see what had happened; women and children were frightened, and the party broke up in panic.

Omaha history started with a bang, and it continued that way. Spectators, settlers, merchants, and others who had been eagerly awaiting the opening of the land hurried across the river to build a city. Streets a hundred feet (thirty meters) wide were staked out near the ferry landing opposite Council Bluffs. Lots were sold for twenty-five dollars each. In July, 1854, the first building in Omaha was constructed of logs at what is now the corner of Twelfth and Jackson streets. Soon the community had a hotel and restaurant, and by the end of the year there were fifty settlers.

Youthful Omaha shared in much of the slam-bang history of the frontier—gunfights, fortunes lost and made in gambling, and quick

The Omaha skyline.

pioneer justice. One rope was made to do the work of two in a famous double lynching. The rope was thrown over a tree, with a culprit suspended from each end.

Justice and progress were not long in coming, although the state's first court case had "comic opera" overtones. The case concerned the theft of half a cheese from Douglas House, one of Nebraska's first hotels. An early account says: "The jury brought in a verdict of not guilty, at which the landlord flew into a rage and ordered the jury out of the house. This was a most serious situation, as there was no other place to stay. Finally, however, by the persuasion of friends and the return of the half cheese, the landlord relented, and thus ended the first lawsuit in Nebraska."

Soon steamboats were docking almost every day, bringing emigrants.

Ground was broken for the transcontinental railroad at Omaha in 1863. From that moment on, the future of Omaha as one of the country's great transportation and commercial metropolises was assured.

Much of early Omaha history centers around its most enterprising families, such as the Creightons, Cudahys, Brandeises, Kountzes, and Paxtons. The present city has plenty of energetic boosters. One of the most unusual organizations anywhere is the Knights of Ak-Sar-Ben. The organization began in 1894 when a group of Omaha businessmen decided that some kind of an annual festival, such as New Orleans's Mardi Gras, would be good for their city. They hit on spelling Nebraska backward as the name of their organization. The annual Ak-Sar-Ben Ball and Coronation has become one of the country's best-known annual festivals. The organization sponsors sports events, livestock shows and rodeos, races, and other events in its Ak-Sar-Ben Field and Coliseum. The Ak-Sar-Ben 4-H Baby Beef Show is said to be the most outstanding of its kind in the nation.

Races at the Ak-Sar-Ben festival are sponsored by Omaha businessmen.

Omaha's civic auditorium covers four city blocks. It includes an arena, a music hall, an assembly hall, and an exhibition hall.

Omaha's Joslyn Art Museum is a leading midwestern cultural center. The museum was donated by Sarah Joslyn in memory of her husband George. The four-million-dollar building is itself a work of art. More people visit and support the Joslyn Museum in proportion to population than any other art museum in the nation. It has a fine permanent collection and also offers outstanding special exhibits.

Another principal cultural institution is the Omaha Symphony Orchestra.

The Omaha Medical Center has risen around the University of Nebraska College of Medicine. It includes a doctors' office building, the Bishop Clarkson Memorial Hospital and Nursing School, and complete facilities for specialized treatment of children. Children's Memorial Hospital, one of the largest in the Midwest, is served by 265 doctors. Special care is given to convalescent and handicapped children.

The City Emergency Hospital building was willed to the city by Anna Wilson, known as the Queen of the Underworld. The city debated for some time before accepting the gift.

Omaha is headquarters for the world's largest health and accident insurance company—Mutual of Omaha. The city has come to be known as the Hartford of the West, since more than thirty-five insurance companies are located there.

Offutt Air Force Base, just south of Omaha, is headquarters for the Strategic Air Command (SAC), America's main line of air defense.

An entirely different kind of institution, yet equally well-known, is Boys Town, near Omaha. Started by Father Edward J. Flanagan, its renown was spread when the movie *Boys Town* was made, starring Mickey Rooney and Spencer Tracy.

Omaha is the site of the College World Series—the championship baseball playoff of the National Collegiate Athletic Association.

Poignant reminders of the pioneer past can be found in modern Omaha. There is the Mormon cemetery, site of one of the Mormon's winter camps, where six hundred of the Saints were buried.

One of the most unusual and touching monuments depicts a Mormon father and mother standing mute and dejected over the open grave of their dead child.

A well-known collection of Americana is contained in the Museum of the Union Pacific Railroad. It features a fine display of Lincoln material, including a replica of his funeral railroad coach, as well as other relics of the railroad's history.

The city is well endowed with gardens and parks. Mount Vernon Gardens is a replica of the estate of George Washington. It overlooks the Missouri River Basin site passed by Lewis and Clark in 1804. Riverview Park, with its zoo, is another popular feature. Levi Carter Park now rests on a piece of Iowa that was cut off by the Missouri River and left in Omaha in 1877. Just a few miles from the heart of Omaha is Fontenelle Forest, the largest tract of virgin timber in Nebraska. This wilderness area has been recognized by the federal government as one of the top natural history sites in the nation.

THE REST OF THE EAST

"Nestled in the rolling hills above the Missouri River, Brownville is a living embodiment of the past," according to *Nebraskaland* magazine. "Untouched by the dash and turmoil of today, Brownville retains the restful atmosphere and quiet charm of nineteenth century America. Its drowsy Main Street, dusty side roads, and steamboat architecture have survived today's mad rush."

To enhance Brownville as a tourist attraction, the historical society has restored several old buildings. These include the Carson House, equipped with post-Civil War furnishings; the Muir house; Furnas home; grist mill; and Captain Bailey's house, now a free museum.

Each year Brownville holds a festival to celebrate old times. The people dress in period costumes. There are horse-drawn buggies. A flea market is held on Main Street, and candle making, rug weaving, and flax spinning are demonstrated.

Beatrice is the site of the Homestead National Monument of America. The land of Daniel Freeman, who claimed to be the

The fiddler's contest at Brownville is only one of the events held during the annual festival that celebrates old times.

nation's first homesteader, was set aside in 1936, through the efforts of Senator George W. Norris and others, as a "proper memorial emblematical of the hardships and the pioneer life through which the early settlers passed in the settlement." Visitors can view the Palmer-Epard homestead cabin, with furnishings and tools used by the pioneers.

Each year Beatrice celebrates Homestead Week in June. The trial of Wild Bill Hickok is recreated in rip-roaring fashion. Top cowboys vie for heavy purses at the rodeo, and there are parades, carnivals, and contests.

Nearby Fairbury celebrates every August with its "Echoes of the Oregon Trail" pageant. A cast of two hundred brings to life many of the storied characters of the region.

Another historical pageant honors Princess Alice Blue Cloud, daughter of Red Cloud. The princess died and was buried on a bluff of the Republican River, looking down over the city that bears her father's name. Her favorite pony was buried beside her. Each year on the Fourth of July, the community recreates the events of the princess's life and honors the passing of the Indian era. Chief Red

Apple canning at Kearney. The old fort has been restored and visitors are welcome at what is now Fort Kearney Historical Park.

Cloud was the last great warrior chief of the Ogallala Sioux. He held two important war councils on the site of the city that bears his name.

Red Cloud, Nebraska, also remembers its most famous daughter, writer Willa Cather. The Willa Cather Museum is housed in one of the town's original buildings.

Hastings' House of Yesterday is an unusual museum for a community of its size. It features the "world's largest collection on the rare whooping crane," historic Nebraska articles and agricultural implements, old-time fashions, and exhibits of thirty-five habitat groups, along with many others. Also located in Hastings is the J.M. McDonald Foundation Planetarium, gift of the foundation to the city. In 1877 Hastings won election as county seat. However, until a group of Hastings citizens stole into rival Juniata, put the county records on lumber wagons, and scurried back with them to Hastings, it was the county seat in name only.

Near Minden is Pioneer Village, buildings housing a collection of more than thirty thousand items of pioneer Nebraska. Antique autos, horse-drawn vehicles, and one of the world's largest collections of farm tractors may be seen there. The buildings include an original sod house, Pony Express station, and old schoolhouse.

Fort Kearney was moved to present Kearney in 1848 to protect the Oregon Trail. This important outpost has been restored as Fort Kearney Historical Park, and much of it may now be seen by visitors. Because of its central location, Kearney at one time hoped to become the capital of the United States.

According to Arnie Garson, "One of the most magnificent commercial and cultural centers of its day was located at Kearney." This was the Kearney Opera House, the only building between the Missouri River and Denver with a stage large enough for major productions.

The founders of Grand Island also dreamed that their city might someday become the national capital. Grand Island did not achieve this goal, but it did manage to become the third largest city in Nebraska.

Leo Stuhr, son of a pioneer Grand Island family, contributed 115 acres (46 hectares) of land and $500,000 to create the Stuhr Museum and surrounding Land of the Prairie Pioneer. American architect Edward Durell Stone designed the museum building to rest on an island in a man-made lake. On Pioneer Prairie a trail takes the visitor past a recreated Pawnee village, an old Grand Island settlement, a nineteenth-century farm, and a turn-of-the-century village with both business and residential districts. Additional features are an agricultural demonstration area, a botanical garden, and an outdoor amphitheater.

One of the principal buildings of Grand Island is Grand Island Roman Catholic Cathedral.

Near Grand Island is Stolley State Park. Here in 1864 William Stolley built a kind of private fortress, which he called Fort Independence, to protect his family and nearby settlers from the Indians. The fort contained an underground stable 88 feet (27 meters) long.

There are relatively few American Indians left in Nebraska. Winnebago is a small Indian town, headquarters of the Winnebago Indian Agency.

At Bancroft the life and work of Nebraska poet laureate John G. Neihardt are remembered in the quaint one-room cabin that he used for a study. The room is filled with manuscripts, first editions, and other mementos of the poet. On the grounds is a Sioux prayer garden like the one Neihardt described in *Black Elk Speaks*.

Fremont was named for General John C. Frémont. Its municipal auditorium, seating 3,500, is unusual for a city of its size.

One of Nebraska's best-known estates is at Nebraska City. This is Arbor Lodge, the former home of J. Sterling Morton. The fifty-two-room Morton mansion was given to the state by the family and is now a part of Arbor Lodge State Historical Park. Here each year the founder of Arbor Day is honored on his birthday, April 22, with a tree-planting ceremony. Another Nebraska City landmark is John Brown's cave, a major station on the underground railroad. The first high-school building in Nebraska was built at Nebraska City in 1864.

WESTERN NEBRASKA

Hewitt in his dugout,
Sought a name for his P.O.
He suggested several
But Uncle Sam said "No."
His two boys went a hunting,
An Indian bow brought back.
'Twas broken, but they hung it
Upon the dugout shack.
He shouted when he saw it,
"This name will surely go."
And Uncle Sam okayed it—
That's why it's "Broken Bow."

Nebraska farmland in the fall.

Right: James Bordeaux's fur-trading post at Chadron has been completely restored and is now the Museum of the Fur Trade.
Below: The buffalo herd at Fort Niobrara National Wildlife Refuge (below) numbers more than two hundred.

This doggerel may not be exactly accurate, but it is true that the town got its name when Wilson Hewitt found a broken Indian bow. At Broken Bow is the only two-story sod house still standing in the United States.

Broken Bow is the eastern gateway to the vast Nebraska Sandhills region. George A. Peterson wrote in *Prairie Paradox:* "There is no other geographic spot like it in the world—20 counties of north-central Nebraska—where lush green grasses now cover once-naked, windblown dunes of desert sand; where a land of taboo has become a land of plenty.... Hard-bitten soldiers and cowboys feared a land they believed to be without water, and they swapped tales of people who had gone in but never came out....

"Not until 1879 did E.S. Newman, whose ranch stretched from the Niobrara at Valentine west to Wyoming, start using the lake country. Even then it was by accident. It was, in fact, out of sheer desperation that an attempt was made to rescue a few of the 6,000 head of cattle stampeded by a March blizzard into the mysterious hills.

"In April after the snow had melted, 12 courageous men rode into the interior. After five weeks of roundup they brought out 3,000 more cattle that had drifted in ... —9,000 beeves ... fatter and sleeker than those at the home ranch." From that time on, the Sandhills became a favorite of cattlemen.

At Valentine is Sawyer's Sandhills Museum, where exhibits depict the romance of the region. Near Valentine is Fort Niobrara National Wildlife Refuge, which has a museum of natural history. A now rare prairie-dog town is preserved there. Visitors are fascinated by the twice-yearly roundup of the buffalo herd, which numbers more than two hundred. The calves are tagged, branded, and turned loose to roam. The refuge also has a herd of 150 Texas longhorns.

Rushville still remembers the visit of President Calvin Coolidge. One of the most popular pictures of the president was taken near Rushville, showing Coolidge in an enormous cowboy hat.

During the 1860s James Bordeaux operated a fur-trading post at Chadron. His post has been completely restored on the original foundations and is now the Museum of the Fur Trade. Exhibits present the story of trapping as Bordeaux and other mountain people knew it. The museum features one of the finest collections of Northwest Indian trade guns found anywhere.

Chadron State Park is the largest state park in Nebraska.

The name of Crow Butte near Whitney recalls a tale of Crow braves who took refuge on the butte. Their Sioux enemies besieged the rock. However, the Crow cut apart their blankets, tied them together, and the young men escaped down the unguarded, steep side. To keep the Sioux from becoming suspicious, the old men of the Crow danced and sang noisily all night. When the Sioux discovered they had been tricked, they let the old men go. Soon they made a long-term peace with the Crow.

The fort founded at Crawford in 1874, in the midst of the Indian troubles, has become Fort Robinson State Park with a museum of natural and physical history. North of Crawford are the Nebraska Badlands. They are not so well known as those of the Dakotas, but they have a wild beauty all their own. A part of this region has been set aside as Toadstool Park, where the gnarled landscape casts an enchanting spell.

The fossil beds near Agate have become Agate Fossil Beds National Monument.

In the Alliance cemetery are the graves of Jules Sandoz and his wife. Sandoz, the vibrant horticulturist of the Sandhills, is memorialized in his daughter's *Old Jules*.

Scottsbluff, site of a national monument and museum, was named for Hiram Scott, a fur trader who died in the region in 1828. His death is described by Washington Irving in *Adventures of Captain Bonneville:* "Scott was taken ill; and his companions came to a halt, until he should recover health and strength sufficient to proceed. While they were searching round in quest of edible roots, they discovered a fresh trail of white men, who had evidently recently preceded them. What was to be done? By a forced march they might overtake this party, and thus be able to reach the settlements in safety.

"Should they linger they might all perish of famine and exhaustion. Scott, however, was incapable of moving; they were too feeble

82

to aid him forward, and dreaded that such a clog would prevent their coming up with the advance party. They determined, therefore, to abandon him to his fate. Accordingly, under pretense of seeking food ... they deserted him and hastened forward upon the trail. They succeeded in overtaking the party of which they were in quest, but concealed their faithless desertion of Scott, alleging that he had died of disease.

"On the ensuing summer, the very individuals visiting these parts in company with others, came suddenly upon the bleached bones and grinning skull of a human skeleton, which, by certain signs they

The strangely shaped rocks at Toadstool Park (below) are located in the Nebraska Badlands.

University Hill and Carnegie Hill, at Agate Fossil Beds National Monument

recognized for the remains of Scott. This was sixty long miles from the place where they had abandoned him; and it appeared that the wretched man had crawled that immense distance before death put an end to his miseries."

When railroad surveyors came upon the wagon wheel marking the grave of Rebecca Winters, a Mormon woman who died on the westward trail, they built a fence around the spot and routed the railroad around it. A granite marker now stands as a memorial to all mothers who died on the trail.

One of the most famous landmarks of the trail was spiked Chimney Rock, between Gering and Bayard. It thrusts its peak 350 feet (107 meters) above the Platte River.

84

Sidney, Big Springs, and Ogallala were among the rip-roaring towns of western history. Twenty-three saloons once crowded a single block of Sidney. The town's saloons, dance halls, and gambling houses never closed. Shootings were so common they attracted almost no attention. At a dance one night someone was shot; the corpse was propped up in the corner. The dancing went on and a second corpse joined the first. Only after a third corpse joined the other two did the party come to an end. Today Sidney is a peaceful farm trading center.

At the end of the cattle trail, Ogallala "roared loudly enough to provide a decade of scripts for television westerns." One historian reported: "Gold flowed freely across the tables, liquor across the bar, and occasionally blood across the floor as a smoking gun in the hands of a jealous rival or an angered gambler brought an end to the trail of some unfortunate cowhand on the stained boards of 'Tuck's' Saloon. . . . Its gaming tables were never empty, its bar never dry,

A reproduction of Front Street, Ogallala, one of the old "Wild West" towns.

and its ladies never too preoccuped but what the newly arrived cowhand found a welcome.''

According to George Peterson ''Ogallala residents knew on sight the faces of some of the West's most notorious gunmen. One was Doc (Daniel C.) Middleton, Nebraska's most infamous outlaw. Whether he deserved it or not, he got credit for all the livestock-stealing crimes within five hundred miles (eight hundred kilometers) of his Sandhills hideout. Another was professional gambler Luke Short, whose name was made the day he outdrew Jim Courtright, Texas' famed quick-shot artist.''

Many frontier characters are buried in the Boot Hill Cemetery of Ogallala. Today at Ogallala there is a reproduction of Front Street, where shoot-outs are staged for visitors even more regularly than the real thing occurred.

At Arthur, thirty-four miles (fifty-five kilometers) north of Ogallala, is Pilgrim Holiness Church, built in 1928 with baled hay. Another interesting church was the one at Keystone, with a Catholic altar at one end and Protestant at the other.

No one had ever robbed a Union Pacific train until notorious outlaw Sam Bass and his gang stopped one at Big Springs station. They greedily helped themselves to three crates of gold pieces—an unexpected stroke of luck. The passengers were lined up and made to give up their valuables. When Sam saw that one man had only one arm, he gave back his watch and money. A Texas cattleman stashed his $3,100 under a chair, and Don Fretwell palmed his big diamond in his boot. Nonetheless, Sam and his gang pocketed $1,300 in addition to the gold.

Near Lewellen was one of the most heartbreaking places on the western trails. This was Windlass Hill, a very steep descent from the bluff top to the river bottom. An English traveler in 1849 wrote that ''no one spoke for two miles, the descent was so breath-taking. . . . Riders dismounted and led their horses, wagon wheels were locked and the wagons steadied with ropes.'' There were many casualties—men, beasts, and equipment.

The Memorial Art Gallery at Chappel is noteworthy for its fine collection of etchings by such artists as Rembrandt and Whistler.

McCook is noted as a meat-packing center. It bears the name of General Alexander McDowell McCook. It was the home of Senator George W. Norris.

Near Maxwell is Fort McPherson military cemetery. Bodies were brought there from more than twenty western military posts after the Indian wars ceased. Buffalo Bill was once stationed there as a scout.

North Platte is the metropolis of central and western Nebraska. There the north and south branches come together to form the Platte River. For thirty years North Platte was home to frontier showman Buffalo Bill. In 1882, Buffalo Bill put on a Fourth of July celebration. It was such a success that he was inspired to bring together a large number of trick riders, sharpshooters, and other experts in the lore of the West. With this group he created the Wild West show for which he later gained world fame. That first Fourth of July show is claimed to be the world's first rodeo, though Texas disputes the claim. Each year North Platte stages its Buffalo Bill Blowout in honor of the showman.

Buffalo Bill's Scouts Rest Ranch at North Platte is open to the public. In the gigantic barn where the wild west acts trained, yellowing posters acclaim the show. The rafter supports are carved in the shape of gun stocks. The nineteen-room mansion may be viewed by visitors, and there is a museum of period furniture and Buffalo Bill mementos.

In Memorial Park is another museum, the D.A.R. Museum, a small cedar cabin. It houses early utensils, relics from Custer's last stand, and other reminders of the early West—the proud heritage on which Nebraska has built such a varied present.

Handy Reference Section

Instant Facts

Became the 37th state March 1, 1867
Capital—Lincoln, settled 1856
State motto—*Equality Before the Law*
State nickname—The Cornhusker State
State bird—Western meadowlark
State tree—Cottonwood
State flower—Goldenrod
State grass—Little blue stem
State gemstone—Blue agate
State fossil—Mammoth
State song—"Beautiful Nebraska"
Area—77,407 square miles (200,483 square kilometers)
Greatest length (north to south)—211 miles (338 kilometers)
Greatest width (east to west)—430 miles (693 kilometers)
Highest point—5,430 feet (1,655 meters), western Banner County
Lowest point—825 feet (251 meters), southeast corner Richardson County
Geographic center—Custer, 10 miles (16 kilometers) northwest of Broken Bow
Highest recorded temperature—118° F. (47.8° C.), Geneva, Hartington, and
                                        Minden
Lowest recorded temperature—-47° F. (-43.8° C.), Camp Clarke
Population—1,570,006 (1980 census)
Population density—20 persons per square mile (8 persons per square kilometer)

Principal cities—	
Omaha	311,681
Lincoln	171,932
Grand Island	33,180
North Platte	24,479
Fremont	23,979
Hastings	23,045

You Have a Date with History

1541—Coronado crosses Nebraska plains
1598—Oñate enters region
1682—French claim entire western region
1720—Pedro de Villasur killed by Indians
1738—Mallet brothers visit Nebraska
1804—Lewis and Clark explore Nebraska
1806—Pike explores Nebraska
1811—Wilson Price Hunt crosses state
1812—Fort Lisa established
1819—Stephen Long expedition marks Nebraska as "desert"
1823—Bellevue becomes first permanent European settlement

Opposite: Fort Falls at Fort Niobrara.

1833 — First Nebraska mission established
1842 — John C. Frémont crosses Nebraska
1847 — Mormon trek begins
1849 — 49ers cross Nebraska on way to California
1854 — Nebraska becomes a territory
1863 — Daniel Freeman claims first homestead
1867 — Statehood; railroad completed across Nebraska
1871 — University of Nebraska opens
1887 — William Jennings Bryan comes to Nebraska
1898 — Trans-Mississippi Exposition, Omaha
1902 — Nebraska National Forest established
1904 — Kincaid law permits 640-acre homesteads
1917 — America enters World War I, in which 47,801 Nebraskans serve
1932 — Capitol dedicated
1934 — Nebraska becomes only unicameral state
1941 — America enters World War II, in which 120,000 Nebraskans serve
1957 — Governor's mansion completed; new Omaha charter
1963 — Nation's first sodium graphite reactor opens near Lincoln
1963 — Sheldon Memorial Art Gallery completed
1967 — Nebraska celebrates its statehood centennial
1973 — Gerald R. Ford, Omaha native, becomes vice president of the United States
1974 — Ford succeeds to the presidency

Governors of The State of Nebraska

David Butler 1867-1871
W.H. James 1871-1873
Robert W. Furnas 1873-1875
Silas Garber 1875-1879
Albinus Nance 1879-1883
James W. Dawes 1883-1887
John M. Thayer 1887-1892
James E. Boyd 1892-1893
Lorenzo Crounse 1893-1895
Silas A. Holcomb 1895-1899
William A. Poynter 1899-1901
Charles H. Dietrich 1901
Ezra P. Savage 1901-1903
John H. Mickey 1903-1907
George L. Sheldon 1907-1909
Ashton C. Shallenberger 1909-1911
Chester H. Aldrich 1911-1913
John M. Morehead 1913-1917
Keith Neville 1917-1919

Samuel R. McKelvie 1919-1923
Charles W. Bryan 1923-1925
Adam McMullen 1925-1929
Arthur J. Weaver 1929-1931
Charles W. Bryan 1931-1935
Robert Leroy Cochran 1935-1941
Dwight Griswold 1941-1947
Val Peterson 1947-1953
Robert B. Crosby 1953-1955
Victor E. Anderson 1955-1959
Ralph G. Brooks 1959-1960
Dwight W. Burney 1960-1961
Frank B. Morrison 1961-1967
Norbert T. Tiemann 1967-1971
J. James Exon 1971-1979
Charles Thone 1979-1983
Bob Kerrey 1983-

Thinkers, Doers, Fighters

People of renown who have been associated with Nebraska

Aldrich, Bess Streeter
Astaire, Fred
Beadle, George W.
Bessey, Charles
Blackbird (Chief)
Brando, Marlon
Bryan, William Jennings
Cather, Willa
Cody, William F. (Buffalo Bill)
Cook, James H.
Creighton, Edward
Creighton, John
Dawes, Charles G.
Flanagan, Edward J.
Fonda, Henry

Ford, Gerald R.
Hanson, Howard
Houston, James (Jim)
Joslyn, George A.
Judd, Walter
Lloyd, Harold
Morton, J. Sterling
Neihardt, John Gneisenau
Norris, George William
Piper, Edwin Ford
Sandoz, Jules
Sandoz, Mari
Sheldon, A. Bromley
Stuhr, Leo
Taylor, Robert

Annual Events

April—Arbor Day, Nebraska City
April—Five-State Art Show, Scottsbluff
April—1884 Days Celebration, Valentine
June—Homesteaders Days, Beatrice
June—College Baseball World Series, Omaha
June—Old Times Day, Osceola
June—Nebraskaland Days, Lincoln
July—Princess Alice Blue Cloud Pageant, Red Cloud
July—Alice Blue Cloud Pageant, Crystal Lake
July—Oregon Trail Days, Gering
July—Black Powder Shoot and Parade, Holbrook
July-August—Indian Pow-Wow, Winnebago
August—Echoes of the Oregon Trail Pageant, Fairbury
August—Omaha Indian Pow-Wow Council, Macy
August—Buffalo Bill Blowout, North Platte
August—Nebraska Czech Festival, Wilber
August—Hay Days Celebration, Atkinson
September—State Fair, Lincoln
September—Old Home Town Festival, Brainerd
October—Ak-Sar-Ben, Omaha
October—World's Championship Rodeo, Omaha
December—"Christmas Island Lighting Night," Grand Island

Index

92

93

94

PICTURE CREDITS

ABOUT THE AUTHOR

With the publication of his first book for school use when he was twenty, **Allan Carpenter** began a career as an author that has spanned more than 135 books. After teaching in the public schools of Des Moines, Mr. Carpenter began his career as an educational publisher at the age of twenty-one when he founded the magazine *Teachers Digest*. In the field of educational periodicals, he was responsible for many innovations. During his many years in publishing, he has perfected a highly organized approach to handling large volumes of factual material: after extensive traveling and having collected all possible materials, he systematically reviews and organizes everything. From his apartment high in Chicago's John Hancock Building, Allan recalls, "My collection and assimilation of materials on the states and countries began before the publication of my first book." Allan is the founder of Carpenter Publishing House and of Infordata International, Inc., publishers of *Issues in Education* and *Index to U. S. Government Periodicals*. When he is not writing or traveling, his principal avocation is music. He has been the principal bassist of many symphonies, and he managed the country's leading non-professional symphony for twenty-five years.